No Mind No Prob'

No Mind No Problem

No Mind

No Problem

No Mind No Problem

No Mind No Problem

Investigate Your Mind, Relax into Pure Being and Discover Your Real Self with Natural Pure Awareness Meditation

By

Ramaji

No Mind No Problem

No Mind No Problem

ISBN-10: 1490440518
ISBN-13: 978-1490440514

Ramaji.org

Ramaji Books
San Diego, California
Email: satsangwithramaji@gmail.com

No Mind No Problem

Books By Ramaji

The Spiritual Heart

Waking Up As Awareness

You Are Everything

The Tao Of Non-Doing

Awaken Your Inner Shamanic Healer

Warning From Kali 2013

No Mind No Problem

"What is called mind is a wondrous power existing in the Self [natural pure awareness]. It projects all thoughts. If we set aside all thoughts and see, there will be no such thing as mind remaining separate; therefore, thought itself is the form of the mind. Other than thoughts, there is no such thing as the world."

— Sri Ramana Maharshi

No Mind No Problem

Table of Contents

Meditation for People Who Know How to Meditate

Journey to the Heart Of Truth

Natural Pure Awareness

How to Meditate on Natural Pure Awareness

Wake Up Background and Liberate Foreground

Be a Warm Neutral Friend to Your Thoughts

The Anatomy of Thought and Sitting Inside Your Story

The Myth of the Mind and the Prisoner of Thought

Investigate the Thinker and Expose the False Center

The Narcissistic Core and the Architecture of the Ego

Meet the Author

No Mind No Problem

Meditation for People Who Know How to Meditate

I showed this book to a few dozen people before publishing it. Most were my spiritual students, but not all. I wanted to know what they liked and what they didn't like about it. I wanted to know what worked for them and what didn't work for them.

The feedback I got back said plainly that the most useful part is cultivating a kinder, gentler relationship to your thoughts. Others told me the chapter that explained the ego I-thought in terms of the toxic narcissistic core and the levels of self-defeating egocentric self-indulgence was unique and quite helpful.

On the negative side, I was informed by a professional educator I deeply respect that this book did not work as a course. It started out with the big picture, then broke it down piece by piece. I was told it should be linear and gradually build on what came before. In other words, start small and get bigger instead of start big and then look at the different pieces of the puzzle.

I was told that if you were a beginning student of meditation, it was too advanced. I was told that if you were an advanced student of meditation, you probably didn't need it. In a recent email to a student, I jokingly said "This is a book on meditation for people who do not need a book on meditation."

Based on this feedback, I considered revising it. In the end, I decided to leave it just as it is. The truth is this is how this book wants to be. This is how it came out and this is how it wants to stay.

It has brilliant strengths and glaring weaknesses. It is not a "course," but I never meant it to be a course. What I would like it to be is an experience. That is why it starts off with the big picture. Perhaps you will have an "aha" moment — sort of like when the vastness of the Grand Canyon comes into view for the first time.

Anyway, here it is. It is how it wanted to be. I organized it as best as I could for you.

The bottom line is that your natural state is who you are and it has NO thoughts in it at all. It never did and it never will. It is Ramana Maharshi's Self. It is Nisargadatta's Absolute. It is Shiva Consciousness. It is Universal "I" Consciousness. It is Mahamudra. It is Zen Master Seung Sahn's "only don't know" mind aka "nothing-mind." It is Zen Master Bankei's "Unborn Buddha-mind."

You Are That... and You Are That right here right now at this very moment. Enjoy.

May You Discover the Deep Natural Diamond Peace of Your Real Self,

Ramaji
San Diego, California
Ramaji.org

No Mind No Problem

Journey to the Heart of Truth

When I was 16 years old and living in a suburb of Los Angeles, California, I had a lucid dream that changed my life. In this dream, I was in India. I was with a yoga guru who spoke to me in Sanskrit. He took me through many hatha yoga postures, then I ended up sitting in padmasana, in lotus posture.

Then next thing that happened was literally mind-blowing. Everything exploded and my sense of separate self that I had been feeling in the dream dissolved totally and completely into a blissful peaceful Ocean of White Light.

When I woke up the next morning, my Kundalini was awakened. I also had amazing psychic powers. I'm not going to go into details, but I will say having this sudden unexpected Kundalini awakening was very difficult. It was hard enough just being a teenager. The extremes of emotion from the Kundalini were astonishing.

I managed to muddle my way through this crisis. I was in high school. I was still living with my parents. Though I knew next to nothing about yoga, meditation or Eastern religion, I knew that enlightenment was real and that it was better than anything else.

I had a reading by a gifted spiritual psychic. She told me that I would have to wait a long time. She predicted that I would not see fruition of my spiritual yearnings until my 40s or 50s. She said I would have to be very patient.

It turned out she was right. To a teenager, waiting for the fulfillment of your heart's desire until you're 40 or so sounds like an eternity. Yet I sensed this delay was in my destiny.

What this experience did is force me to recalibrate everything in my inquisitive young life. Now life was transparent. It was just going through the motions. All the usual things that a young man could get excited about didn't amount to a hill of beans.

I had experienced a blissful transcendental Light that made everything else meaningless. All that life offered was now nonsense. Life was a cosmic joke, but I didn't know the punchline.

It was a paradoxical situation. It made me laugh. It made me cry. It made me doubt God. It made me love God. But one thing was for sure. I could never go back.

In the 1970s, I got involved with some marginal gurus. I made mistakes and I learned from them. I became a vegetarian. I started doing hatha yoga every morning.

In the early 1980s, I ended up living in a Sivananda ashram in Hollywood, California. It was there that my spiritual practice began to stabilize. The assistant head of the yoga center was studying Vipassana meditation. I learned about it from her.

I took up Vipassana ("Insight") meditation in earnest. I would meditate one or two hours a day plus practice mindfulness while walking. At first, I just did things by the book. I followed the instructions very precisely. Then I discovered that because I was always making tactile contract with something during the day, I could remain in a state of mindfulness in the world via the sense of touch. All day long I was making continuous contact. I was touching the phone when I held it. My back was against the chair as I sat in it. There was always a mindful kinesthetic contact I could access.

The modern school of Vipassana that I studied focused on noticing the fleeting body sensations. Once your acute perception enable you to detect the movement of these bodily sensations, you shifted to perceiving the fundamental impermanence (Pali: *anicca*) of these ever changing body sensations. This became possible only when concentration was built up and maintained.

I had the good fortune to study with the Venerable Shinzen Young. He is a wonderful human being and a brilliant enlightened spiritual teacher. He has achieved much success as a meditation master. His success is well-deserved.

Even though he taught a contemporary approach based on science, I was drawn to the classic Buddhist text *Vishuddimagga* (Path of Purification). I studied it and learned about the classical stages of the unfolding of impermanence. This traditional sequence of spiritual events or milestones on the road to Nibbana (Nirvana) is described by a few modern Vipassana teachers, too.

Even though I was living in a huge Western city, I went through these stages exactly as described in this old book. It was amazing. They had every step right.

These stages culminated precisely as the old book had predicted in the flash of Nirvana (Pali: *Nibbana*). I was doing very slow walking meditation on a driveway behind the main meditation house in busy noisy smoggy hot downtown Los Angeles when it happened.

This transcendental event was unmistakeable in its character. It was not my imagination. It, too, was just as described in these ancient books from another time, country, religion and culture. My experiences prove that the Buddha's teachings are universal.

Since Vipassana had been good to me, I stuck with it for seven years. But there came a time when it began to feel restrictive and limiting. There was not anything "wrong" with it. It is a brilliant practice. My clock of destiny was ticking. It was time to move on.

Advaita and Vipassana totally agree on the universal factor of impermanence as being key. Vipassana is the Buddha's version of Advaita Self-inquiry meditation.

When I encountered Kali Ma, I was deep into my Vipassana meditation lifestyle. I was living in a yoga center. She appeared to me at the Sri Ramakrishna Advaita Vedanta Temple in Hollywood, California.

I was meditating there alone and the statue of Kali they keep up at the front moved. I saw Her walk by. Then I smelled the most lovely fragrance of sandalwood. Then She started talking to me.

Mother Kali has a very distinct way of talking. She talks like she is in total command. She talks like she is the general and you are the private.
She said to me, "You are mine. I own you. Your body is mine. I am in complete control of your destiny."

I was surprised at how at ease I was with this sudden turn of events. I calmly replied "Okay, I believe you. If that is true, then what is next?"

Whispering in my ear again, Kali added "If you agree to this spiritual contract with me, I can guarantee that you will attain spiritual liberation in this lifetime. You must be willing to surrender unconditionally to me. Then I will control your life circumstances in order to guarantee your realization. Anything less than total surrender is unacceptable. What is your decision?"

She didn't say that exactly. She is a Divine Mother of few words! That was the essence of Her proposition.

Without hesitation, I said "Yes. I surrender completely to you. I give my life over to you. My life is yours."

She smiled. Then just as quickly as She had appeared, Her Presence was gone. The sandalwood evaporated.

When I asked somebody on the grounds about the Temple being open with the statue of Kali out on the stage there, he acted surprised. The next time I visited the temple Her statue had been moved behind an iron fence. Kali was in jail! I laughed out loud.

In early 1988, out of the blue the persistent thought came to me that "My last name has the name of God, Ram, in it, so my guru is going to have Ram in his name." The thought just kept repeating over and over.

At this same time, I experienced a strange but not unpleasant metallic taste in the middle of my tongue. I have not felt that taste before or since. I believe it was an impression from Akasha (the etheric element).

A few months later I saw Ramesh's picture in a Hollywood paper. I instantly knew it was him. I intuitively knew with total certainty that meeting him was my destiny. He was going to change my life.

So what did I do? I decided to wait a year because I wanted to have one last year of living with the ego! Looking back at it, it was a bizarre reaction. My thought at the time was "I'm not quite ready."

Fast forward to my encounter with Ramesh Balsekar in Solana Beach, October, 1989. I saw him later at several group meetings. This first time was at "Joe's Crab Shack" with about 50 people.

I have never loved a man like I loved him. I felt that he was my spiritual father. I love my biological father totally. He was my first spiritual mentor. The spiritual connection with Ramesh transcended everything. The feeling was like an ocean of love. I would cry and cry tears of joy.

The last event I went to took place in Pennsylvania, USA. On one of the days, I noticed two men talking loudly as Ramesh spoke. They were expressing doubt about Ramesh's realization. When I told Ramesh, he shouted at me that what they were doing was none of my business. It felt like pure Grace and Love to me.

I finally had a chance to talk to him one on one. He was hanging out after giving a talk to the large group.

When I walked up to the small gathering around him in the back of the room, he abruptly stopped talking to them and turned to me. I still remember the force of his penetrating gaze as it locked into my eyes. There was no escape from those magnificent eyes!

I said something about how much I loved him. Then I told him that I wanted to come to India to be his servant. He looked deeply and genuinely shocked.

"Oh, no," he said, "that is total nonsense! You should not be lingering around. I have given you everything I can give you. Go study with other teachers if you like. Or just do whatever you want. It won't matter. I have given you all I can. Now you must move on with your life. I cannot help you anymore."

I said "Thank you" and reached out to give him a hug. He accepted. It was a magical embrace where time seemed to stop. The joy and gratitude you feel with the person who has revealed the Self to you simply cannot be described.

Even though this was the last thing I wanted to hear, I intuitively knew he was right. I never saw him again after that meeting. It was his last visit to the United States. He lives on in my heart and in my life.

My spiritual quest for ultimate freedom then took me back to Sri Nisargadatta Maharaj and Sri Ramana Maharshi. I studied their teachings all over again and practiced the unique meditations they had revealed.

In 2006, the Kundalini completed Her journey to the Crown chakra. I experienced a vision of Mt. Kailash (a mountain in the Himalayas sacred to Lord Shiva). A secret passageway from the Crown down to the Heart on the right called Amrita Nadi was revealed to me. It was like a secret tunnel that went down inside Mt. Kailash. It went from the Crown to the Heart.

The Amrita Nadi blazed with life-transforming light. It was the ultimate spiritual event of my life. Amrita Nadi ("channel of immortality") and the causal Heart on the right are in the teachings of Sri Ramana Maharshi.

The awakening of Amrita Nadi has been described as "the light of a thousand suns." The world turns translucent and disappears in a blaze of Divine Light.

When the world returns, it is not the same world. That world is gone forever. There is only the one supreme Self. You can still perceive the world and function in the world, but for you the world is literally the universal Self. There is only the Self.

As I write this, I am reminded of the spontaneous Kundalini event of 1966 when I was a teenager. I have come full circle. The glorious Light that was revealed in 1966 was the Light realized in 2006.

I went on to lead my first non-dual Satsang retreat in Toronto in the summer of 1994. Since then I have worked privately with individuals and groups to facilitate their awakening. I chose to avoid public life.

Responding to a divine decree, I moved to San Diego in June, 2012. I was given a "direct order" to begin my public mission as a spiritual teacher of non-duality, Advaita and enlightenment. Jai Guru Dev!

Many Blessings in the One Self, Ramaji

No Mind No Problem

Natural Pure Awareness

In this book, I will show you how to investigate your own mind and self-liberate it into its natural relaxed and open state. You will be able to see for yourself exactly how your mind works. After you see that, then you will be able to be free of it. Once you are free of your mind, then you will enjoy your natural state.

In your natural state, you cannot find your mind. That is because you don't really have one. What you do have are thoughts. These thoughts come and go, but thoughts coming and going are just thoughts coming and going.

When you look for your mind, all you will find is thoughts. That's because there is no mind.

You probably believe you have a mind. If so, where is it?

We can talk about your thoughts, but we cannot talk about your mind. Mind is just a concept.

That would be okay but because people think they have a mind, they do not see that their thoughts just come and go. People think they are a thinker and this thinker has a mind. Because they think they have a mind, they think they have problems.

They think that they have to control thoughts and this becomes a big struggle. Even though they are supposed to own these thoughts, somehow they cannot control them.

28

But if you do not have a mind like that, then all you can have are thoughts that come and go. If you do not have a mind like that, then you have no problems.

No mind. No problems.

In your natural state, you are happy and you feel completely free. There is no effort to this as it is what you are.

Your mind was obscuring your natural happiness. After you are done clearing up the mind, then all of this will be obvious to you. You will be able to enjoy your life and take things as they come.

Your natural state is the enlightened state. Dig up the I-thought, the narcissistic thinker who is the root of your mind. Get rid of him and then you will just have thoughts to deal with now and then. These thoughts are like clouds in a big empty blue sky. They do not bother you and they add to the sky.

Every now and then there is a storm, but the storm is okay, too. It adds a rich flavor to your existence. It is a celebration of what it is like to be human. All of it is accepted. The war is over. You enjoy a tremendous ease and effortless sense of well-being. You enjoy deep lasting peace.

Your Beliefs, Your Thoughts and Your Mind

In order to do this work on yourself, no special beliefs or background are needed.

You can be of any religion. You can have no religion.

If you have a mind, then you qualify.

If you would like to investigate and see for yourself the real nature of your thoughts and your mind, then this is definitely for you.

Since you are having the experience right now of having a mind, the statement that you do not have a mind may not make much sense to you.

What I am pointing to is how your belief in having a "mind" as some kind of self-existing force or thing is not to your advantage. Yes, you have thoughts. But the impression of unity that you experience with your thoughts that come and go all day long is due to the unbroken presence of natural pure awareness.

The "thinker" or apparent organizing center behind the mind is false.

It is natural pure awareness that creates, maintains and dissolves thoughts. Natural pure awareness is able to perform all the functions of the mind and then some. You will see this for yourself when you get there.

For now, even if it doesn't make much sense, consider letting go of the concept that you have a "mind." Instead, allow for the possibility that what you have, quite obviously, is thoughts. There is something, a presence or space or ground, that these thoughts arise from and return to.

Think about your "mind" as just thoughts like clouds coming and going in the wide open sky of natural pure awareness. This is a very good way to think about this experience of thoughts that we are all having each and every day.

In sum, thoughts are fine and they are not the problem. Let go of this notion of mind and look instead for the ever present source of thoughts. This source of thoughts is not a thought. Nor does it have any thoughts in it.

This mysterious source of thoughts which is beyond, below, behind and prior to the so-called "mind" is what I am calling natural pure awareness.

You Are Natural Pure Awareness

You are natural pure awareness.

In Advaita or non-duality, you are known as the Self. In Buddhism, you are called Buddha Nature. In Christianity, you are referred to as Christ Consciousness.

I am saying you are natural pure awareness because when you hear about the Self or Buddha Nature or Christ Consciousness, your reaction might be "Oh, those are just concepts. I don't know about such things in my everyday life."

Maybe this is true. But if you are reading this book right now, then you will have to agree with me that you are aware. In this very moment, you do have awareness.

You are aware. Because you are aware, then everything else in your life is possible.

You have thoughts, emotions, a physical body. You have clothes to wear, food to eat, a place to live. You probably have a car, a phone and a computer, too.

But if you were not aware of these things in the first place, you would not be able to use them. You would not even know they exist.

You might be a billionaire. If you are not aware of your billions of dollars, of what use are they to you?

Awareness is the most fundamental fact of our human existence.

It is also obviously true that awareness is natural.

Suffering arises when your experience of your awareness is not pure.

Returning to the natural purity of unconditioned awareness is what this book is about.

I wrote this book because when you are able to experience yourself as this natural pure awareness, you are then able to experience how you are naturally free under all circumstances and conditions.

You discover that your very nature is to be happy, peaceful and loving.

Since these qualities are your very nature, they do not come and go. You are able to enjoy them at all times. Your personality and how other people perceive you is another matter, but that is not the subject of this book.

This book is about attaining personal freedom for yourself and gaining liberation from the shackles of the conventional thinking mind.

After you achieve your freedom and know yourself to be unbounded and unlimited as natural pure awareness, then dealing with your personality and other people will be effortless and no big deal to you.

Why Natural Pure Awareness Gets Ignored

The funny thing is that because awareness is so fundamental and universal, it gets ignored.

Unless there is a problem on the road, people do not think of the street beneath their feet. It is there so that they can go here and there and do this and that. The road is a means to an end.

So even though awareness makes everything else possible, it is not given credit for what it is doing.

Please take a moment right now. Take a moment to become aware of your awareness. Be aware that you are aware.

Ask yourself "If I did not have this awareness, if I was not aware that I exist, if I was not aware of my thoughts, of my emotions, of my body, of this world, then what would I have?"

The answer, of course, is that you would have nothing. But without the support of awareness, you would not even be aware of this nothing!

Notice the Space in Your Room and Around the Objects in Your Room

Right now you are probably sitting in a room. Most likely you are sitting or lying down.

There are various objects around you. Perhaps there is a rug on the floor. Perhaps there is a table and chairs. Perhaps there are pictures on the walls.

The point is that these things are here and they are what occupy your attention. If there are pets or people moving around in this room, the fact that they are moving and changing in some way will pull your attention to them. This is what happens in your inner landscape, too.

Looking at the room you are in right now, please instead choose to be aware of the empty space. Become aware of the empty space that is generously providing a place for all of these objects.

When you choose to become aware of the background of natural pure awareness that is always present in your inner experience it is a lot like this. Objects (your thoughts) are moving in your mental room (inner space of pure awareness).

As soon as you become aware of the space in your room instead of the objects in your room, you automatically shift from being preoccupied with the objects in your foreground to being suddenly aware of the unbroken continuous background in which these objects are appearing.

This choice may not make much of a difference for you in your experience of your physical room when you switch from preoccupation with the objects in the foreground to the wide open space that is their background. But it will make a huge difference when you are able to do it with your inner or subjective objects and your inner or subjective space.

The shift from foreground to background will instantly liberate these objects a little bit. When this happens, you may experience a sudden and enjoyable feeling of ease or release. This openness feels good!

The Art of Total Acceptance

If your bias is that you need to manipulate your subjective experiences, that you need to control your thoughts and emotions, then you have an investment in changing them.

As a result, total acceptance of what is happening to you in this moment will escape you.

The rejection of your now experience is taking place one thought, one emotion and one state at a time. The outer ecology reflects the inner ecology. If you want to be able to be at ease with your life and enjoy it to the fullest, then stop rejecting the moment to moment events of your inner life.

As within, so without. If you would like your outer world, your "without" experience, to be rich, harmonious and full, then embrace your inner life moment by moment.

Warmly greet each thought and emotion with open arms. No matter what its appearance, demeanor or story, invite it to sit down with you and break bread with you.

Become good friends with all of your rogue, stranded, abandoned, isolated, rebellious, confused, wandering and troubled "parts" and thoughts. Invite them back into your inner family. You are the mother and father who gave them life. Give them a good home.

Thoughts Are Creating Your Problems, But They Are Not the Problem

To say you are natural pure awareness is actually redundant because awareness is always pure.

But people get their experience of this pure awareness mixed up with their thoughts and negative emotions. So it seems then that awareness is just a little background light illuminating the stage of human action. The so-called "mind" appears to dominate us.

Thoughts, emotions, the body and human actions take center stage and grab almost all of our attention.

I would like to help you restore your pure awareness so that you experience it in all of its unbounded glory. This pristine awareness is without thoughts. It has no thoughts in it at all. It never did and it never will.

You may not see it now, but it is thoughts that are creating all of your problems. No matter what your problem, the reason that it is a problem for you right now is your thoughts.

Actually, that is not quite correct. It is okay to have thoughts, but when they are out of control, you have a problem. It is okay and even beautiful to have birds.

37

But when the birds multiply like crazy and fill the sky, apparently blotting out the sun, then birds have become a problem.

Likewise, when thoughts multiply like crazy and apparently blot out natural pure awareness, then thoughts have become a problem.

A bird here and there, a thought here and there, is not a problem. The bird or the thought is seen for what it is in reference to the wide open sky, the eternal background, of natural pure awareness.

Natural Pure Awareness Is Free Because It Is Always Without Thoughts

Natural pure awareness is free because it is always without thoughts. Thoughts are what bring limits. It never has any thoughts. So it never has any limits. No thoughts. No limits. That is its secret.

Natural pure awareness is like the big wide open blue sky.

There may be clouds in the sky or there may not, but to the sky it makes no difference.

When you are established in natural pure awareness, then you are like the sky. There may be thoughts or there may not be thoughts, but to you it makes no difference.

You do not need thoughts in order to live. Thoughts need you in order to exist, but you do not need thoughts.

You exist with or without thoughts. You are natural pure awareness, the stainless timeless thought-free stateless state.

After you gain freedom from the illusion of a mind that is separate from you, you will discover that all of the functions that you thought were being performed by your mind were in fact being performed by natural pure awareness. Natural pure awareness was doing everything all along.

So when the illusory construct called the mind gets dismantled, it is discovered that you still have everything you need and nothing that you don't need. The mind is just thoughts. There is no organizing entity, no thinker, behind it. As long as you believe there is a thinker behind the mind, you will suffer the consequences of your error.

When you observe the behavior of your thoughts closely with compassionate clarity, you will discover that you have thoughts, but you do not have a mind as you had believed. Your belief in an independent, free-standing mind that was out of control that you needed to control was the result of not observing closely how your thoughts arise in the moment.

You did not look at this situation for yourself and so you did not see it as it actually is. After you investigate and see the situation for yourself, your doubts will be cleared and you will understand how to be free no matter what happens. You have all the tools right now to do this investigation.

It is the most important thing that you can do with your life. Investigate your own mind and find freedom in your natural state. After you find it, it will be effortless to maintain it. It is what you are.

No Mind No Problem

How to Meditate on Natural Pure Awareness

The reason you investigate your mind is to discover the true source of your thoughts. You have heard that you have a mind but so far all you have been able to find is thoughts.

When you finally investigate these thoughts you will discover that the foundation for the arising of your thoughts is not the so-called "mind." Instead what you find is a wide open benevolent spacious awareness. This natural pure awareness is what is aware of your thoughts. It is the real source of your thoughts.

You discover that not only is this natural pure awareness what enables you to be aware of your thoughts, it is also the good kind loving mother of your thoughts. When you see this for yourself, then you are set free from the limiting illusion of the mind.

Then you know that there are only thoughts coming and going in the context of benevolent wide open intelligent wholeness.

Thoughts arise from this wise benevolent neutral mother space and return to this wise benevolent neutral mother space. This kind generous supremely neutral great mother space for your thoughts is this natural pure awareness.

Meditate Every Day

It is good to meditate every day. If you can't meditate every day, then meditate as often as you can.

If you cannot sit down and meditate, then snatch moments during your day where you pause to stop and study your mind. Even a few "stolen" minutes like this can make a huge difference in your life.

A good period of time to meditate is 20 minutes. If you have half an hour, that is better. If you have an hour a day, that is even better. But like I said, even five stolen minutes is better than none.

Some people divide their hour of meditation a day into half an hour in the morning and half an hour before they go to bed. Everybody is different.

So find a meditation schedule that you can stick to and keep it going. Even five minutes a day is better than doing nothing. The five minutes can be right after you wake up or before you go to bed. It can be during your lunch break at work.

When you understand meditation, there is nothing simpler or easier. The reality is that you are always in meditation. It is what you are. That is because this natural pure awareness quite literally IS the state of true meditation.

In deep meditation or through a spontaneous awakening or from a combination of both, you eventually arrive at a profound unshakeable silence.

When this elegant imperturbable silence becomes permanently established as your home state, then you live in this beautiful silence all of the time.

Then thoughts and emotions and sensations can come and go, but they will not disturb this organic silence. This is not just a state of having a quiet mind. This silence that you are was here all along.

This is a challenge for people to understand. If my mind filled with busy thoughts is so noisy, then how can this profound silence also be here? Even so, it is right here and that is what you eventually recognize. You do not need to invent this silence. It is already the source of all of your thoughts.

So I talk about natural pure awareness and say it is different from the so-called "mind." This natural pure awareness and this ultimate silence are one and the same. They are different names for the same thing.

When you think you are the thinker, that you are the mind and have a mind, then thoughts are a problem.

When you know you are natural pure awareness and that your true nature is beautiful bottomless silence, then thoughts are not a problem for you. They come and go and it is okay. All of your functioning is taken care of by natural pure awareness. This was always so.

The difference now is that you experience this truth for yourself. Natural pure awareness is like your mother. She is always taking care of you. Life becomes very simple. There is still pain and discomfort now and then, but life itself is good.

Or life is like a series of delicious delightful meals served to you by good friends. There is an atmosphere of generous good will and effortless benevolence.

Every now and then there is something you don't like all that much, but overall the experience is enjoyable and sublime. The overwhelming flavor is one of harmony with others and fulfillment within.

Life delivers an endless parade of fascinating surprises. You enjoy life from the benign perspective of the whole, not the frightened fretful perch of a beleaguered alienated stranded part.

You automatically focus on what is important in the moment. You effortlessly ignore that which is not important in this moment. This is your secret for living a happy life and it is as easy as breathing.

But in this moment, you are not aware of the silence. But you are aware of your awareness. So for that reason, we will start with your awareness. We will uncover the truth about your awareness.

When this truth is uncovered, your awareness will emerge and come forward as natural pure awareness without any conditions or limits. This is noble true awareness in its regal and royal state finally free from the callous shackles of claustrophobic thought.

When you see that this natural pure awareness is who and what you are and you stabilize in it, then you will realize that you are always naturally happy and free.

Your happiness, peace, joy and love never originated from your thoughts. They originated from your true nature or core essence as natural pure awareness. They are not separate from you and they never were.

To be happy is your very nature, but you must see through the blindfold of the thinking mind filled with unruly thoughts in order to know this for certain. You see things as they really are, and since they really are that way — that natural pure awareness is the source and truth of everything — that seeing is enough.

The Revelation of Awareness

Natural pure awareness is the state without thoughts. It is the natural state, the ground state in which all of your thoughts come and go. If natural pure awareness was itself just a thought or made up of thoughts, then thoughts could not freely come and go within it.

In order for life to go on, there has to be something that is always here, always open and always supporting everything.

46

That something cannot be a thought, an emotion, a body or a separate self.

It has to be able to stay wide open at all times. It has to be able to accept and embrace everything, no matter what it is.

Whatever you see happen in our world, whatever you know has happened inside of you or inside of another person, that event could have happened only because this invisible ground, this universal support, was there and embraced that event with wide open arms.

This unconditional support, this all embracing ground, is this natural pure awareness.

This is why I keep saying "This pristine natural pure awareness has no thoughts in it. It never did and it never will." This point is important!

It is important because as soon as something has thoughts stuck in it, thoughts stuck to it, thoughts defining it, thoughts refining it, it is now stuck in time and space. It is now a "thing."

It is now an event, a subject, an object, a happening with a time and a place. It is localized. It is time-bound and space-bound. It is born and it will die.

This is the power of thought. It takes the Infinite and tries to define it. It tries to make the Infinite definite. Since the Infinite cannot be limited, it does not end up with the Infinite. It ends up with a conceptual object that it can play with and manipulate.

But the Infinite, being infinite, goes along with the mind's game. In the fullness of time, in the realm beyond time and space, all is resolved. The Infinite is infinitely patient. So it waits until the mind is bored with all of its games.

Then natural pure awareness, the Infinite within the finite human experience, comes forward and claims its rightful place as the untouched source of thought that is itself always beyond thought, without thought and free of thought.

To Meditate on Natural Pure Awareness, Start with the Breath

Meditating on natural pure awareness is very simple.

The purpose of meditating on natural pure awareness is to become aware of awareness itself just as it is.

Right now, you are aware of the objects that your natural pure awareness is illuminating.

For example, you are aware of your thoughts, your emotions, your sensations and your experience of self. But you are probably not in this moment aware of awareness itself.

If you are getting inundated by thoughts, then you will need to do something to calm the mind first. The practice of following the breath in and out of the nose is good for calming the mind.

If you have 20 minutes for meditation today, then for the first five minutes you can follow the breath in and out of your nose. You want to be right there physically with your attention at your nostrils. Feel the air moving in and out. Notice the physical sensations of the air making contact with your nose.

Some people find following the breath at the belly easier. They can feel the belly rise and fall as they breathe. If that is easier for you, then do that. Again, pay attention to the changing physical sensations.

After following the breath in the nose or at the belly for awhile, begin to emphasize the out-breath. Gently extend the exhalation. With each exhalation, let go. With each exhalation, let everything go. Let body go.

Let mind go. Let self go. Let everything go. Let it all go.

Eventually, you will find yourself resting in deep silence when you breathe out. Allow this and enjoy it, but do not force it. As you rest in this spacious silence at the end of the exhalation, the in-breath will naturally arise.

The breath rebirths itself without struggle or effort. Automatically a new cycle of breathing begins. Enjoy this spacious restful silence. When the in-breath takes place, enjoy that, too. Breathing is an amazing, wonderful life-giving miracle.

The purpose of this preliminary calming step is not just to reduce the number of thoughts you are having. It slows down your thoughts and introduces you to the spiritual joy of spaciousness.

This method of following the breath in and out was taught by the Buddha. It is also taught by Lord Shiva in the beginning of his *Vijnana Bhairava Sutra*.

This simple yet powerful meditation technique is thousands of years old. The original talk by the Buddha describes the 16 steps for using this breath meditation to attain enlightenment. It is called "The Anapanasati Sutta" or "Breath Mindfulness Discourse."

The Method for Meditating on Natural Pure Awareness

The method for meditating on natural pure awareness is to become consciously aware of your awareness. This awareness is present in your present situation, whatever that situation is. This is because if you are aware of the situation, then awareness is available.

In order to become conscious of your awareness, you will need to vividly notice that is at this moment in the background. You want to bring it into the foreground.

Natural pure awareness meditation can be done sitting in meditation every day. You can choose to set aside, say, one half hour a day to become fully conscious and aware of your ever-present awareness.

I would say that is very good. It is also very good to make being consciously aware of natural pure awareness something that you do all day every day. You can do it anytime anywhere.

Meditating on natural pure awareness and becoming consciously aware of natural pure awareness are the same thing.

Natural pure awareness is already the thought-free state of ultimate meditation. When you meditate on natural pure awareness, you begin at the beginning, but this beginning is also the end.

You begin at your destination. You begin with natural pure awareness. You end at natural pure awareness.

Since awareness is present as the ground for every experience that you will ever have, then every experience is potentially an opportunity to become consciously aware of this natural pure awareness.

Natural Pure Awareness: the Sitting Meditation

Let's say that today you can sit for half an hour.

STEP ONE: CHOOSE TO RELAX

If you like, you can spend the first five or ten minutes doing a calming meditation.

Earlier, I suggested following the breath in and out of the nose for that.

After your "mind" has calmed down some, you can switch gears.

STEP TWO: NOTICE WHAT YOU ARE AWARE OF

In this moment, what are you consciously aware of?

For example, let's say you are upset with somebody in your life.

As you know, this is uncomfortable, even painful.

Maybe you are running a movie about this situation.

Maybe you are remembering what they said or what you said.

Maybe you are just feeling upset and unhappy.

This is what you are consciously aware of right now.

STEP THREE: TENDERLY INVESTIGATE YOUR NOW SPACE OR GROUND OF AWARENESS

So let me ask you this.

How exactly is it that you are AWARE of these things?

How exactly is it that you are able to NOTICE these things?

How exactly is it that you are able to be CONSCIOUS of these things?

Allow yourself to feel upset and be unhappy.

Do not interfere with that. Do not judge it. Do not try to change it.

Now ask yourself something like "What is the space in which my subjective events are happening?"

Or "Where is this space in which my subjective events are taking place?"

Instead of asking in terms of SPACE, you can ask about your natural pure awareness as GROUND.

"What is this wide open ground on which my subjective events are happening?"

Or "Where is this wide open ground on which my subjective events are taking place?"

This can be a verbal inquiry at first, but it quickly evolves into a silent questioning or investigation. It becomes an earnest intuitive gesture, a sincere heart-felt investigation into the depths of subjective time and space.

STEP FOUR: MAKE AN ENTRY IN YOUR JOURNAL

Your spiritual or meditation journal is a valuable asset. If you like, it can just be a desk or book calendar. The most important thing to do is make a note that you meditated that day. You meditated from this time to that time for a total of whatever minutes.

If you have the time and space to make a note about your insights, experiences and questions, feel free. But the main thing is to document the fact that you meditated.

If you can find somebody who will be your meditation buddy, that is fantastic. You will be accountable to this person and they will be accountable to you. They can call you up or meet with you once a week and ask you "Friend, did you meditate every day like you told me you would?"

Then you ask them the same thing. This is powerful. It is common to feel lost and powerless when first taking up meditation.

Jesus said "When two of you are gathered in my name, I will be there." The same can be said of meditation. The true name of Jesus is Silence.

This journey is into inner space. It is the greatest and most rewarding adventure of all. This is the supreme quest deep in the heart of the final frontier. This is diving into the hidden realm of the highest secret.

Natural Pure Awareness Meditation Is Not the Same as Witnessing or Watching Thoughts

If you have done some meditation, then this may sound like witnessing or watching thoughts.

It may sound like noting or another mindfulness skill. I agree that it sounds similar to that, but it is not that.

The difference is that you are not trying to witness, watch, note or be mindful. What you are doing is simply and totally allowing what is happening on the inside of you to just happen.

There is a very specific reason why you do not want to introduce the concept of witnessing, watching, noting or being mindful. You already have and are the perfect witness. That perfect witness is the natural pure awareness itself.

By allowing your content to just be exactly the way it is, whatever it is, that will be enough to encourage your pure awareness to come forward and make itself known to you.

What tends to happen when you propose a witness, watcher or something else that is doing that job is that it becomes a concept.

This concept gets in the way. Because now you have a new concept to put your attention on, natural pure awareness does not come forward like it otherwise might have done.

So please do not introduce any new concepts. You do not need any concepts to meditate on natural pure awareness. You are already doing what you need to do, which is experience your changing subjective content and emotional events just as they are.

The difference is now you will be experiencing your subjective content with a new commitment.

For at least the duration of your meditation, you will NOT interfere in ANY way with ANY your stuff.

You are going to let it run on EXACTLY as it is appearing. You are not going to do anything about it.

What would natural pure awareness do about it?

It would do nothing about it. It would embrace it totally and support it absolutely.

That is what it is doing effortlessly and beautifully right now in YOUR subjective sky of experience!

The purpose of natural pure awareness meditation is to bring natural pure awareness FORWARD so that you can know it and experience it more directly exactly as it is. If you mess with your foreground content, then your natural pure awareness will just stay in the background like it always does.

The way to bring natural pure awareness from your background into your foreground is to start BEING LIKE natural pure awareness. You intentionally bring natural pure awareness into your now experience.

You do this by consciously not interfering with your experience in any way. You accept and allow it just as it is without judgment. Pure awareness will naturally begin to display itself and come forward because the non-judgmental space has been made for it.

Start with the Open Space Heart of Reality

Instead of looking for what is real, you are starting right here now from the open space heart of reality.

Natural pure awareness is the wide open space heart of always here always now reality.

It is always here. It is always now. It is always open. It always supports everything.

It never goes away. Listen to it. That sound of silence is it. That gap between thoughts is it.

That moment right after you did something and before your ego I-thought steps in to falsely claim credit for it, it is there in that moment.

Thoughts are its clothes. They hide its beauty. Take off the clothes. See the translucent glory of the naked radiant body of ever new natural pure awareness.

You can start right here in natural pure awareness. Allow it to expand. Allow it to come forward.

Rest with contentment in that natural pure awareness. Find spontaneous joy not caused by thought in that natural pure awareness. Be free in that natural pure awareness.

There are no thoughts in this natural pure awareness.

There are no problems in this natural pure awareness.

No stress, no pressure, no conflict, no contraction, no confinement. You are free. You are your own master.

You do not feel any limitation to your freedom. At last, you are finally being your true self.

Be This Natural Pure Awareness.

Be Your True Self.

You Are That Now.

Wake Up Background and Liberate Foreground

Most of us are very near-sighted with our thoughts. We get extremely close to them. As a result, we cannot see them as they actually are.

You could be in a big beautiful luxurious room but if you stand with your nose to the wall all you will see is the wall. You will not be able to see all of the elegant things in the room.

It is very powerful to step away from this myopic claustrophobic position in relationship to your thoughts. When you move away from them just a little bit and give them some space, it is amazing how things open up. Only a little space is needed for big changes to take place.

It is not natural for thoughts to accumulate and gang up on you. This is the result of you neglecting your thoughts and not paying attention to them. When you give them the attention they deserve and study them respectfully to find out where they come from and where they go to, you learn an amazing truth.

You find that it is none other than yourself as this wonderful wide open naturally abundant pure clear awareness that your thoughts arise from and return to all day long.

The Purpose of Natural Pure Awareness Meditation

The fewer the number of thoughts that you are having, the better it is for you.

The slower the thoughts that you are having, that is also better.

Why is that?

The purpose of meditating on natural pure awareness is to study the nature of thoughts and arrive at a correct understanding about the real nature of the mind.

When you look at thoughts as they come and go and see them as they really are, then natural pure awareness automatically comes forward and reveals itself. The confusing notions of "mind" and "thinker" get fully dissolved and completely resolved.

As long as you are fascinated by the drama and glitter of your thoughts and take them at face value, natural pure awareness stays in the background. It is obvious you are being entertained by the many possibilities that all of these thoughts represent.

Since you are preoccupied with your thoughts and content with the experience you are having, there is currently no need for natural pure awareness to come forward and reveal itself. You are not showing enough interest in it as it is for it to do that for you right now.

It is the nature of natural pure awareness to not interfere. Instead, it allows and it accepts. It does this without limits or conditions or favorites.

As a result, it does not step forward. Since it does not step forward, it does not draw attention to itself.

But when you get tired of being a slave to the mind, when you are ready to rise up and shake off the shackles of your domineering arrogant tyrant mind, then you will get very interested in this pure natural awareness and its true role in everything.

Natural pure awareness is happy with you if you are happy with your experience, whatever that is right now. In fact, natural pure awareness is happy with you even if you are unhappy with your experience.

When you are unhappy with your current experience, it may happen that you start to investigate your experience. You become seriously curious about it. You want to know how this experience that you are having right now that you don't like very much got created in the first place.

If you then stick with your investigation and trace your current experience all the way down to its deepest roots, you will find that the hidden secret ground for your now experience is this effortlessly free natural pure awareness.

For most people, natural pure awareness is sitting in the background and they do not notice it. They do not notice it because they are paying attention to something else.

What they are paying attention to are their thoughts, their emotions, their sensations and their separate self. They are paying attention to them because they are moving and changing. That grabs the attention.

When you turn your attention to just the thoughts that you are having as you are having them, and you let go of your other concerns, including your survival concerns and your worldly concerns and your thoughts about other people, then you begin a journey of discovery unlike any other.

It is the greatest journey of all for it will take you beyond time and space.

It takes you to your true self. Your true self is unbounded, unlimited and unconditioned.

Your true self is free. Your true self is this natural pure awareness.

You are already that. That is the reason you can realize it. If you were not already that, then no amount of effort or thinking could make you that.

Effort and out of control thinking come from forgetting that you are that. When you realize that you are that natural pure awareness, effort disappears, thinking changes profoundly and you enjoy impeccable boundless freedom.

Thoughts still arise but now there is no thinker. In fact, there never was a thinker and you never had a mind like you thought you did, but this is something you will just have to see for yourself.

If you do the work, you will see the truth about yourself, your thoughts, your mind, your life, your relationships, other people, the world, God and the universe. It will all become crystal clear to you.

Life will be like a big blue cheerful sky on a bright sunny day. Everything is open and whatever shows up is just part of what you are. It will be natural for you to welcome it. After all, it is your very self. It is you.

Let Go of Watching the Watcher (Pounce on It!)

Meditation is often taught as passive "just watching" meditation. This is okay at the beginning, but you will want to go beyond just watching. Passive witnessing will not take you all the way. Assertiveness is needed.

Before, you were identified with and involved in your thoughts. The improvement now is that you are just watching them. But there is a step beyond that. When you are ready, it is important for you to take it.

The watcher, who is the same thing as the thinker or the experiencer, is just a thought. When you watch the watcher thought, what typically happens is that you create another watcher thought in order to watch the first watcher thought.

Now you have one watcher thought watching another watcher thought. Then this watcher thought gets watched by another watcher thought and so on. This chain of thoughts watching each other is a dead end.

The solution is for awareness to POUNCE on a watcher thought. You grasp it, embrace it and dissolve it as natural pure awareness itself. You do not "watch" it.

If you just watch it, you create the artificial distance that we call "thought." In authentic awareness, there is no separation. The ISness is everything all at once.

When you successfully "pounce" on the watcher or observer thought, there will be a release of energy.

This energy feels good. It is an intuitive spontaneous state of wholeness and well-being. This is the natural state. It feels automatically complete. It is pure Beingness. It is glorious natural pure awareness.

When You Become Aware of Both Foreground and Background at the Same Time

If it sounds like I am being vague, it is not on purpose.

I do not want to give you a new object to think about or a new goal to strive for.

You are already thinking and striving enough.

Instead what I want to do is invite you to become aware of what you are already doing and what you are already experiencing. I want to invite you to become consciously aware of this ever-present ground of natural pure awareness that is your timeless foundation and source.

This ever-present ground of natural pure awareness does not change.

It has no thoughts or other content in it. That is why it does not change.

At the same time, because it has no thoughts or other content in it, it does not stand out.

You do not tend to notice it. Instead, you tend to notice the moving and changing content.

This moving and changing content, your thoughts, your emotions and so on, is the foreground.

You are now aware of the foreground. Now choose to become aware of the background, too.

The natural pure awareness, which is the stable ground for all of your many changing experiences, is the background.

When you consistently give your attention to this natural pure awareness, it gradually comes forward and becomes the foreground. Then thoughts arise like soft gentle clouds in the pristine translucent sky of natural pure awareness.

The Foreground, the Background and Natural Pure Awareness

The domination of the mind is due to thoughts being too close. It is like they are right on top of you or you are right on top of them. As a result, your perspective is off. When you are able to get some distance from them, then it is much easier to see them as they are and for what they are.

Most people are overwhelmed by their thoughts. On a good day, thoughts behave themselves and there may not be that many of them. Even so, most people are enslaved by and tortured daily by their thoughts.

This is why people like movies, TV and music. They get entertained. They are pleasantly distracted.

While they are being entertained they are not troubled by their thoughts. A good massage or experience in nature can also slow down and reduce thoughts.

What is happening when thoughts are in charge and overwhelming you is that they are taking up the entire foreground of your awareness. All you can see with your inner vision or hear with your inner hearing or feel with your inner sense is thoughts and more thoughts. There does not seem to be an end to them.

They fill up your awareness. They fill up your mind. They dominate your mental landscape and so they dominate your life.

It is a stressful claustrophobic feeling. The monkey of the mind is riding on your back.

Even if you do not ever meditate on natural pure awareness, please walk away from reading this book with this one life changing insight.

Your thoughts are arising within a benevolent neutral space or context or background of some kind, but this benevolent neutral space or context or background is being ignored by you.

Instead, your foreground is filled with thoughts. As a result, you do not notice or even think of this benevolent neutral always present background.

Your life-changing insight is this. You can choose to become conscious of this benevolent neutral background which is always present and always allowing all of your thoughts to come and go.

When you become consciously aware of this benevolent neutral background, it starts to come forward. Your thoughts become less dominant. You easily automatically experience more spaciousness and freedom with your thoughts. Your experience of thinking becomes less pressurized, less problematic for you.

The goal of natural pure awareness meditation is to bring this benevolent neutral background, your natural pure awareness, fully and totally forward. Then awareness and not your thoughts will dominate your inner landscape.

Since your natural pure awareness allows your thoughts to come and go but has no thoughts in it, thinking unwinds and completely relaxes for the very first time.

Then you will have the thoughts you need to live your life. You will not have the thoughts that you do not need. The thoughts that are producing your suffering right now are thoughts that you do not need.

It is easy enough to start looking for this benevolent neutral always allowing and always accepting background to your thoughts. It is simple to start noticing its presence. If your thoughts are coming and going, then there is something they are coming and going in.

You have been told that it is your "mind" that your thoughts are coming and going in, but I am telling you something new and different.

While it is obvious and self-evident to you that you have thoughts coming and going, the reality is that they are not coming and going in your "mind."

What they are coming and going in is your neutral natural pure awareness background. As you study your situation and notice this background more and more, you will see that this is your real situation.

Whether or not you choose to sit down in formal meditation, you can still every day take some precious time to notice this always present background of pure natural awareness and pay close attention to it

As you do this, your thoughts will be fewer and the thoughts that you do have will move slower. You will notice gentle easeful space around your thoughts and enjoy more clarity with your thoughts.

This will improve the quality of your life and deepen your ability to fully enjoy your everyday experiences.

Meditating on Natural Pure Awareness Is Easy and Effortless (You Are Already Doing It)

Just as you do not have to make an effort in order to have thoughts, you do not have to make an effort to be aware of your thoughts. Natural pure awareness is present and aware at all times.

It is present in a totally effortless way. This is obvious and self-evident since it was here all along.

You have never had to make any effort for awareness to be present. It will continue to be here whether or not you choose pay attention to it. That is the nature of this benevolent neutral background, this natural pure awareness.

To have thoughts is effortless and to be aware of the thoughts that you are having is effortless. So meditating on natural pure awareness really is completely effortless. There is nothing to it except to do what you are already doing. You are already having thoughts and you are already aware of your thoughts.

Of course, there has to be more to it since you would like to have a different result than what you seem to be having now. But one of the wonderful things about natural pure awareness meditation is that you are already doing it!

You are already having thoughts and you are already being aware of them. To have thoughts and to be aware of thoughts are both effortless.

Thanks to awareness, you are aware of your thoughts. Without awareness, you would not be aware of your thoughts.

Thoughts are the content of space, like furniture in a room. Even the I-thought, which is also called the watcher, observer, thinker or experiencer, turns out to just be another thought.

Recognize Foreground Versus Background

Everything is possible only because of natural pure awareness. Because of sky, there are rainbows.

The difference when you start doing natural pure awareness meditation is that now you are choosing to bring this benevolent neutral always supportive background awareness into the FOREGROUND of your consciousness. That is the main difference.

Consider a photograph of a group of people in a natural setting. They could be relaxing at the beach, standing on top of a mountain, hanging out on a boat in the ocean.

When you first look at the photograph, it is natural to focus on the people. You tend to zoom in on the people. The people are in the foreground.

What is the environment that these people are in? For example, they are at the beach and the ocean is behind them. You have noticed the people and their possessions. You may not have noticed the ocean.

Natural pure awareness meditation is noticing the people and then noticing the ocean. It is noticing the ocean is the spacious background and noticing the people and their objects are the dynamic foreground.

You are becoming conscious of the difference between the background and the foreground. As you become more conscious of the difference, you naturally bring the background forward. Just by being aware of its contrast with the foreground, it easily comes forward.

This action will be enough to start the process that will reveal the true nature of your thoughts that keep arising and disappearing all day long.

When you are right on top of something, you cannot see it clearly. This is your situation with thoughts.

This natural process of bringing your background awareness into the foreground is enough to unravel your thoughts and expose the limitations of your mind. As long as this natural pure awareness remains solely in the background, you will never know its true nature. As a result, you will never know the true nature of the foreground and you will never know the true nature of your thoughts and your mind.

Consider this. What is the foreground without the background? Can you have one without the other?

It is obvious to us from life that the foreground NEEDS the background. They are two sides of the same coin.

In the world, you take a walk. Suddenly you see a man or a woman in the foreground. They seize your attention. As human beings, we have been taught to put enormous emphasis on other people in our scene.

It could be a car or a beautiful tree or a magnificent horse or something else that really grabs you. None of these things are just floating isolated in space.

They have a background and they simply cannot exist without it. It is our human nature to zoom in on what fascinates us, especially if it is moving and calling attention to itself. This is true of our inner world just as it is true of our outer world.

This changes when you shift your attention to take in the background that is always already there.
Whether it is in the inner world or in the outer world, when you take in more of the vast and majestic background your world is enriched. The foreground object which had been the obsessive focus of your attention is released from your myopic grasp.

It is placed in a healthy context that allows for the easy harmonic fullness of foreground and background.

The oppressive sense that you are overwhelmed, dominated and pushed around by thoughts goes. Your thoughts find their serene natural place in daily life.

Life becomes spacious and self-unfolding. Then you are living life and life is living you moment to moment.

There is nothing to figure out. You live like a happy carefree child. You are ever curious about the next wonder that this endlessly creative life will display. You are ever grateful what this display brings.

There is the release of living with no resistance. There is the joyful celebration of seeing, allowing, accepting, embracing and approving everything exactly as it is.

In the spaciousness of pure awareness, there is only love. No matter what it looks like, it is love. Love is all there is. All there is is love. You are this love.

No Mind No Problem

Be a Warm Neutral Friend to Your Thoughts

It is natural in our society to believe that we must change and control our thoughts. We must improve our thoughts and make them better. In this way, we will improve ourselves and become better.

This is how we think nowadays but it is a subtle trap. The treadmill of endless change and self-improvement is not just exhausting. It destroys our natural powers of self-observation.

If you are convinced that there is something bad, wrong or dangerous about your thoughts and your thinking, then you will take action against them in order to change them. This is an adversarial relationship. Instead of being friends with your thoughts and making them your allies, you are treating them like enemies. Since these thoughts are arising in you all day long, this is important.

Instead, approach your thoughts in a friendly way. Yes, you want to investigate them, but if you are going to investigate them as they are in order to see how they naturally behave, you do not want to go in there like the bull in the china shop. You want your footprint to be gentle and respectful.

When you investigate your thoughts in this way, you will find that they respond to you in a positive way and they open up to you. As you continue with your firm yet gentle investigation, they give up all of their secrets.

They have nothing to hide but if you push them away at the very beginning you will not see them as they are. You will not see where they come from and where they go to. If you want to be free of the tyranny of your mind, then seeing your thoughts as they are is what you have to do.

Resting in Natural Pure Awareness Makes Friends of Your Thoughts

If your thoughts are quickly rushing by and you cannot get a good look at them, then start with calming your mind and slowing your thoughts down. When your thoughts roar through your mind like a big motorcycle gang, you are going to feel that there is not much you can do about your thoughts.

But when one little thought comes wandering in, surrounded by gentle space and easeful openness, illuminated and welcomed by a vibrantly vivid yet profoundly relaxed clarity, it is a different story. Now you can look at this one thought and study it closely in different ways from different angles.

The experience of thoughts arising and disappearing becomes enjoyable and interesting. Each individual thought takes on an appearance akin to an original work of art. Each thought is understood to be unique, creative and intelligently designed. The inner and outer architecture of each thought is made visible and available for scrutiny.

In this way, thoughts become easy to study and their place in human life is understood. The magnificence of thoughts is fully appreciated.
They become wholesome and functional. Success in everyday life is assured. The transcendental truth hidden in the depths of natural pure awareness is profoundly realized and comprehensively enjoyed.

By understanding just one thought better, you will understand every thought better. You will realize that each thought is unique. When you go inside a thought, you see for yourself that it is empty, wide open and undefended at the center.

You find at the heart of each and every thought there is wide open spaciousness. This is pure awareness.

What you are doing when you are just thinking is that you are paying attention to your thoughts, but you are not paying close attention to your thoughts. You are not studying them. You are meeting them at the surface only. When thoughts are arising and you gain space and clarity, it is a tremendous opportunity to understand your thoughts better.

When you meditate on natural pure awareness, you pay VERY CLOSE attention to your thoughts. But at first you do not get closer to them. Instead, you choose to step away from them. You gain some distance from them.

Instead of being right on top of them, you step back and allow there to be some space around them. You look for the background in which your thoughts are arising. You allow for that benevolent background to intensify its uniquely neutral presence. Since it is both inside and outside of your thoughts, this intensification of your natural awareness has life-changing power.

Your immediate goal is to reduce the number of your thoughts. This will happen as you bring awareness forward. As for the thoughts that remain, you want them to be moving slowly. You want them to appear slowly and to disappear slowly.

Then it will be easier for you to see the space around your thoughts and to notice the gaps between your thoughts. This will happen. As you bring awareness forward, your thoughts will slow down on their own.

If you wish to speed up the process of reducing the number of your thoughts and slowing down your thoughts, you can do more of the calming breath meditation. However, the benefit is temporary. This meditation is a tool to help you study your thoughts. In order to arrive at the permanently silent ground behind all thoughts, radical insight is needed.

As you bring awareness forward from the background to the foreground, you study your thoughts and you examine them from top to bottom, inside and out. You look for where they come from and you look for where they go to. In order to see these details clearly, it helps if your thoughts are slowed down and you don't have so many thoughts.

Then you will be able to look at just only one individual thought at a time. You hold onto this thought and study it. You experience the outside of it. Then you go inside of it. This is exploring the whole thought inside and out.

When you have to deal with your thoughts as a crowd, as a gang or a mob, the situation is very different.

They overwhelm you and take charge. It will seem like you have no choice and no control. You have allowed your thoughts to accumulate and gang up on you.

You have allowed the thoughts to rush into your space in a big crowd. If instead they were to come into your space just one at a time, your experience would be different. You would not feel so overwhelmed.

You would be in a position to get to know this thought and become its friend. When you are on friendly terms with a person, they will reveal new things about themselves to you. Likewise, when you get on friendly terms with a thought, that thought will reveal its secrets to you.

If you do not get up close and personal with your thoughts, if you do not become intimate with them, then they will not reveal their deep secrets to you.

You have not asked them so there is no reason for them to show you more than they are already showing you. If you do not first learn their secrets, then later on they will not let you be their master.

What Exactly Is Your Attention? How Are You Attending to It?

Our word "attention" is a fascinating valuable word. "Attention" comes from the Indo-European root word "ten-" meaning "to stretch." Along with *attention,* many other words we use today come from this root.

These words include *tender, entertain, tend* (as in *"tend bar"), intend, contend, suspend, extend, sustain, maintain, lieutenant, tendon, tantra* and *tone.*

The word attention describes an action. You are tending to or attending to something. You are "stretching" out to something, reaching out to it, in order to make contact with it and, most likely, then do something with it.

If we are face to face and you stretch out your arm to touch my face with your hand, you can tenderly stroke my face. In fact, there are even many possibilities within the range of "tenderly stroking" from very light and barely perceptible to gentle and noticeable to firm yet still tender in its quality.

But making contact after you "attend" to my face with your attention can be quite aggressive.

You could slap my face with your open palm.

You could slap my face hard with the back of your hand. You could even ball your hand up into a tight fist and hit my face very hard with your bare knuckles.

When you make your contact via your attention with your inner content, there are so many ways for you to do that. You can be tender. You can be aggressive.

Between the two, there is a whole range of shades and tones and textures for how you make contact with your object. In this work, you want to attend to your inner event with true gentleness.

In natural pure awareness meditation, you want to be deeply aware of the quality of your attention as it makes contact with the inner object of your attention.

You want to be conscious of your attention and you want it to be very tender, very gentle and very respectful of your inner event, of your arising content. You do not want to change your content.

If you change it before you get to know it, you will not be able to see it as it is. If you cannot see it as it is, you will not be able to understand it. You want to be awake and vivid and fully present as your awareness, but not demanding or pushy.

Each moment that you are meditating is a chance to consciously and tenderly attend to the actual content of that moment and the space in which it is arising. Then you will see all of it just the way it is.

Each moment is fresh and new. Each moment is a rare unique experiment in being awake, aware and alive.

Use your power of attention with great tenderness. Be kind, generous, respectful and trusting of your own content. It is important that you make friends with your inner events. Your goal is to get to know them intimately. You want to be respected. So do they.

For this reason, you sincerely do want to be friends with your thoughts, emotions, sensations and separate self sense. When you are gentle with your inner content, it responds to your warmth and tenderness. It opens up like a fresh fragrant flower.

If you attack it blindly and aggressively, it will reject your advance. You will not get to know it.

If you are pushy, dominating and unsympathetic, you will not get to know it. It will want to open to you. if you are judgmental, closed and harsh towards it, it will hide from you. Then you will not get to know it.

If you don't get to know it, then you will never be able to be free of it. The way to be free is to see it as it is and for what it is. To see it clearly, you must love it.

If you are attacking your thoughts instead of making friends with them, if you are pushing them around and pushing them down, chances are that you are afraid of these thoughts. You are afraid of the suffering that these kinds of thoughts have caused you in the past.

Of course, by now you know that such actions are not in your best interest. It is better to approach your thoughts with clarity, tenderness and warmth. You encourage them to reveal themselves to you. They will do this if you let them.

When you stir up the content of your inner space by being blunt and aggressive, when you try to use force to change it rather than gently tending to it, listening to it, seeing it, touching it, being with it and getting to know it inside and out, its secrets will escape you.

Its deep secrets will hide from you. You must earn its trust. Only then will it reveal its secrets.

You must know its secrets in order to solve the puzzle of its appearance in you. So be gentle, kind, generous, open, warm and tender with your inner content and events. Be tender with your thoughts, with your emotions, with your sensations, with your separate self sense. Be tenderly present yet vividly aware. Be filled with enthusiastic curiosity.

Although natural pure awareness is here and now and does not itself change, your ability to be with your thoughts in a tender, alert, vivid and nurturing way, noticing and listening to them without judgment, does evolve. This skill gains in richness, depth and precision until, in a surprise move, your artful attentiveness and the ground of natural pure awareness unite and fuse into one.

Then you are natural pure awareness itself yet you retain your sense of being a person. You are able to enjoy having a unique human identity and a fully featured dynamic personality. You will be able to enjoy this life like never before.

Your experience then is that there is no one else like you in this amazing world of ours, yet you are one with all of it. You could say you get to "have your cake and eat it, too." Once you know it, you will never want to live any other way.

It is like having a life sentence in prison and suddenly you are set free. Not only do you not want to live in that prison again, you never look back.

The reality in front of you is so beautiful it has all of your attention. You are now the free master.

This does not mean you have powers. It means finally you are yourself. You are now more human than before, not less. To be truly human is beautiful.

The good is set free. The bad gets burned up.

Place a Tender Spotlight on Your Thoughts

I have been talking about natural pure awareness as the space or ground for your subjective events.

You have another asset. It is the flexible dynamic expression of this natural pure awareness. This special asset is your attention. It acts like a spotlight. It reaches out and makes contact.

When the focus of your attention is exclusively on your thoughts, then your thoughts dominate.

They take over your horizon. They fill your inner sky. Everything else is blotted out.

The art of natural pure awareness meditation is based on the movement of your attention.

Chances are, right now your attention is myopically focused on your thoughts and emotions. You are so close to them, you are right up on them. As a result, they fill up your perception.

If you are a seasoned meditator, then you may be able to see or feel some space or even lots of space.

But when your thoughts and emotions are so close that it feels claustrophobic, it's like they are right on top of you. This is stressful. Everyday life feels like a burden. You feel distressed and overwhelmed.

You don't notice anything else then other than your thoughts and your emotions. They are the only show in your town. You don't know about other options. You don't know how to get free while performing actions.

When you allow your experience in the moment, no matter what it is, in that allowing there will be some room. Even so, there is a strong habit that most of us have that works against this ability to be allowing.

There is usually the sense that you must do something about your experience when it is painful. You need to "fix" it, to change it, to handle it, to make it better, to make it less, to make it stop, to make it disappear.

If it is pleasurable, you want to enhance it or intensify it or repeat it. Whether it is painful or pleasurable, the notion of just leaving it as it is and letting it just be, good or bad, is not usually at the top of your list.

Returning to the scenario that somebody has said or done something to you that made you upset, you have many options. You can get into the story. You can try to solve it somehow. You can inquire and ask "Who is suffering?" or "Who is this story about?"

Another option, the one you have when you meditate on natural pure awareness, is to do nothing at all about it. Your now situation is a fantastic laboratory for self-discovery. The last thing you want to do is monkey around with it and try to fix it! There is nothing wrong with it! There is nothing to change!

Actually, when I said you do nothing at all, that was not correct. You want to deliberately "do nothing."

It is true that you do nothing at all to change or attempt to change whatever it is that is arising in the moment. It is also true that you do something, but this kind of action, at least in terms of your inner world, may be new to you. You do "doing nothing."

This is extremely subtle. Even though it is extremely subtle, and it may seem very close to doing nothing at all, it is profoundly liberating and decisively powerful.

So what do you do?

First, you make sure you do not interfere in any way with anything. This means if new thoughts arise with the purpose of changing your thoughts or emotions that you are having right now, you do not oppose them or try to stop them or try to change them.

For example, the thought might arise that you "should not" be having this experience. Since it is obvious that you are having the experience, it is clear that in this moment you are meant to have it. Any kind of "should have" or "should not have" is some kind of judgment.

If "should" statements or judgmental thoughts arise, you allow them, too. They, too, have a right to exist. They, too, deserve your respectful attention and loving investigation. These judgment thoughts are perfectly fine. There is nothing wrong with them.

As you sit there and go through everything in this way that spontaneously appears within your experience, you are going to notice that you have freed up some of your attention. Any kind of "free attention" that you can muster up and make use of is consciousness gold.

Natural Pure Awareness Allows Everything

The position in relation to your arising content that you should or have to or need to DO something about your subjective content is a big part of the confusion.

That attitude works to keep provoking new content that then provokes new content and so on. At the root you will find that this defensiveness is based on fear.

Instead, your position, your attitude, is that you do not need to change this content at all. No matter what it is, you do not need to change it.

What you want to do 100% is just be with it, look at it, feel it, experience it, sense it, listen to it, open up to it, be aware of it, notice it and, in general, study it and get to know it better and better. This is the same as unconditionally loving your thoughts, if that helps.

Instead of grabbing onto your thoughts and emotions and gripping them hard in an effort to forcibly move them, manipulate and otherwise change them, you do nothing at all with them. You could say that you are still making contact with them, still attending to them, but you are doing it in gentle sensitive way. You are bringing a subtle tender generous vividly aware deeply caring investigative kindness and openness to them.

If you find yourself getting involved and trying to do something with what is going on in yourself, then you notice that and let that go on. You do not interfere with the interference. Interfering with your subjective events and content is an old habit. It does not go away easily. It will take time to let it go.

Be aware of this tendency to grab onto or push away your arising content. Be aware that you want to change it. Be aware that wanting to change it is based on not knowing what it is in the first place. Because you are afraid of it, you avoid getting to know it.

If you don't like it or you are afraid of it, you will feel like you need to change it or control it or prevent it. The reason you want to change it is that you do not yet understand it.

This action to change the content is aggressive. It is coming from your fear. This aggression clouds up your attention. It stirs things up. It muddies the water. You lose your clarity. You increase confusion. You miss this opportunity to learn.

Even so, if those emotions or inner actions arise, that is okay. Just stay committed to doing absolutely nothing about anything. Remain tender, gentle, trusting. Allow it to arise and to fully be whatever it is.

Meditation is being still, being spacious, being open. Meditation is being this natural pure awareness.

Natural pure awareness never tries to do anything about anything. It allows everything.

Be like natural pure awareness.

It is brilliantly aware, unconditionally accepting, fully present, totally allowing, completely supportive.

It is unconditionally loving. It enjoys a whole-hearted sublime oneness with inner space, time and beyond.

When you are warmly and positively neutral like this, you encourage natural pure awareness. It begins to come forward. As it comes forward, it becomes easier for you to see, feel, sense, listen to and experience it. It gains power and presence. You feel deep peace.

As you make these changes inside, they are reflected on the outside. Your inner tenderness and openness with yourself will be reflected in your outer world as a new tenderness and openness in how others treat you. Your outer life will change for the better without any extra effort on your part. Based on "as within, so without," this is the law of manifestation at work.

NOTE: Regarding the idea that Natural Pure Awareness "allows everything," of course, please apply your common sense.

First and foremost, what this is about is dealing with what is really going on in you and in your world.

This is not escapism. This is the ultimate realism.

Yes, you do chop wood and carry water.

Yes, you do pay your bills and do your laundry.

Yes, you do need to be grounded and practical.

To be "down to earth" comes first. This, too, is being one with "the ground" of Being.

The higher the tree, the deeper the roots.

This is it right here now. Be Here Now.

The Anatomy of Thought and Sitting Inside Your Story

Advanced methods of meditation like pure awareness meditation require significant emotional maturity and psychological stability in the practitioner. You must be boldly, ruthlessly and relentlessly honest with yourself in order to do this kind of meditation.

If you want real results, you will have to face yourself and look at yourself like you never have before. The result will be refreshing, liberating and totally worth it.

In the end, it turns out that your dark old painful prison is entirely of your own making. When you see this – when you REALLY see this! – then you just walk out of it into a bright new happy day.

You don't look back. Your prison cell isn't there anymore. In truth, it never existed. You only thought it did.

The ONLY Tool That You Need Is Your Awareness

The only tool you really need in order to investigate your thoughts and your mind is awareness. Obviously, you have awareness. The next step is to investigate your thoughts. The goal is to investigate them one at a time.

You may find it helpful to keep a written journal. Even a few notes jotted down now and then with the matching date will prove helpful. You will be able to see your progress.

One of the amazing facts about thoughts you will discover is that they are all basically the same. All thoughts have a similar anatomy. Like people, they look different on the outside but on the inside they're pretty much the same.

It is popular today to talk about how we get caught up in our stories. The fact that you are able to tell a story to yourself means you are playing all the parts. This is similar to a dream. You are holding up both ends of the story. You are holding and maintaining at the same time both the subject and the object.

When you become aware that you are holding both subject and object within yourself at the same time, this softens the dualistic fixation and opens it up.

All subject-object experiences take place in and as the unity which is this natural pure awareness that we are. When you notice the pure awareness ground of your story, you awaken its non-dual flavor. This is as true in everyday life as it is in a dream.

Natural Pure Awareness Reveals the Already Present Gaps Between Your Thoughts

As you meditate on natural pure awareness, you will eventually be able to leisurely study just one thought at a time, and then just another thought, and then just another thought. You will notice something new that is very interesting.

What you begin to notice is that there is a SPACE or a GAP between each thought. There is NO connection from one thought to another. You had imagined that there must be one, but now you see that there isn't.

In the beginning, your goal was just to bring the benevolent neutral natural background awareness forward. Now you are enjoying the spaciousness from this pure natural awareness having come forward.

In your enjoyment of that, you are now noticing that your thoughts are arising one at a time. As you study this situation, you see for yourself that each arising thought is unique. It is independent of every other thought. It arises on its own and it disappears on its own. It does not cause another thought. It is not caused by another thought. It arises spontaneously.

Even if you had noticed this before, even if you had noticed that a thought could appear and then there would be a moment before another thought appeared, chances are you did not actually notice that between EACH and EVERY thought there is ALWAYS a space or gap. That gap is always already there.

Eventually, natural pure awareness "comes forward" and presents itself as it really is. You then directly experience and fully enjoy the wide open spaciousness that is the very nature of this kindhearted natural pure awareness. Thoughts come and go like fluffy playful clouds in a resplendent wide open sunny sky.

Then it is very easy to see how thoughts arise and disappear. It is obvious that there are only unique one-time thoughts coming and going. Each thought is its own sublime world. It is self-evident that there is not a mind. There never was anything real, substantial and independent like a so-called permanent "mind."

What there was before and is now is a silent open natural pure awareness in which thoughts effortlessly and spontaneously, even playfully, arise and then disappear.

This situation is wholesome, benevolent and relaxed. It is clearly the natural state. The chronic mysterious underlying tension of that toxic rogue threat called the "mind" is gone. The tyranny of this illusion called the "mind" is over.

You see that it was true all along that the thoughts were coming and going, rising and falling, arising and disappearing in this wonderful wide open graceful space of gentle natural pure awareness. It was always true and it is true right now.

At some point, you even see that these thoughts that rise and fall in natural pure awareness are NOT DIFFERENT from this natural pure awareness. But when you arrive at the point where you see this for yourself, these thoughts are no longer a problem for you. They are just a part of you, of the real you.

Finally, it is also seen that the entity that most people think they are, the separate self, the thinker, the I-thought, this entity itself arises from the abundance of this natural pure awareness.

It too has its origin in this unstained natural pure awareness. It does not originate from the brain or the body. It is the child of this pristine uncaused awareness space.

When this separate self, thinker or I-thought has run its full life cycle as an apparently separate entity, it drops back into this natural pure awareness. It subsides in it and dissolves back into it.

The difference now is that natural pure awareness is able to be itself as it is and consciously enjoy itself at the same time. The evolution of thought as a vehicle for individuation has achieved its transcendental destination. It is then returned to its noble and glorious Source.

The I-thought or thinker or "I am the body" thought or separate self sense or experience of seeming to exist separately from others dissolves into this benign ocean of natural pure awareness. It returns to it and it disappears into it.

Even the so-called "world" turns out to just be another concept or thought. So when the separate I-thought is dissolved into the ocean of natural pure awareness, the apparent world display soon follows.

This you will see for yourself. Then you will have the unbroken experience "There is only this pure natural always free awareness." It is your situation now. You need only become conscious of that fact.

The Anatomy of a Thought

When you look closely at a thought, you will see that it is not substantial.

Not only that, at the center of every thought, there is total openness. At the center of every thought, there is this spacious translucent natural pure awareness. No matter what the thought, no matter how negative or limiting it may appear to be, at the heart and in the center of this thought is naked empty openness, the natural pure awareness.

This is not so easy to see. We tend to take our thoughts at face value. We react to their appearance.

Yet when you do not judge your thoughts as they arise, when you do not run away from them in fear, when you do not push them away because you do not like them, something new will happen.

This new experience is the richness of just being with your thoughts exactly as they are. You learn to hang out with them. You greet them warmly. You are eager to get to know them.

Your thoughts begin to behave differently. Now that you are greeting them with a welcoming attitude, they do not hide from you. They allow their inner workings to be revealed. You will see that most thoughts, like an orange, have a tough or thick textured skin. Once you go inside, you find it is soft and vulnerable. When you go deeper and get to the center of the thought, you find that it has pure pristine nothingness at its core. Its heart is wide open empty radiant space.

Thoughts Do Not Give Birth to One Another

One of the consequences of not being vividly and intimately aware of your thoughts at the moment of their arising is that you will be led to believe that thoughts give birth to other thoughts.

When you are able to observe them closely with great precision, what you will see for yourself is that each thought arises pure and fresh directly from natural pure awareness. It is unique. It is born brand new.

After your new thought rises up from natural pure awareness, it returns back to natural pure awareness. This is the natural cycle of a thought. This is its birth and death. This is true for every thought.

Why is this important?

Let's go back to the example of an argument with someone. When you are running a movie after that event, your inner movie seems to run smoothly and seamlessly. This is an illusion. It is not true at all.

If you slow your inner movie down, you will see that it consists of one thought after another. Each thought is related in content to the previous one, but the thought that rose before did not cause or give birth to the next thought. There is no link or connection between them.

In order to master your thoughts and your mind, you need to see what is going on. Each thought arises and disappears BEFORE another new thought arises and disappears. Then that thought arises and disappears and yet another thought takes its place.

This means that thoughts are not connected to each other. They may be related in content but there is no cause and effect relationship between them.

Have you ever seen for yourself some kind of subtle link going from one thought to the next? This is not likely as there is NO link between the thoughts!

Each thought arises on its own. Each thought is independent and discrete. Each thought is arising from and returning to this natural pure awareness. This natural pure awareness is like the ocean. Each arising thought is like a one of a kind wave on the ocean. This unique thought wave rises up. Then it subsides.

The waves may be coming into the shore of conscious knowing hard, fast and heavy, but they are coming in one at a time. When you patiently pay close attention you will see the individual thoughts as they move.

The Thinker of Your Story Is a Lie and a Liar

The I-thought, the central thinker who is the false core, the pseudo-center, for your stories, is both a lie and a liar. It does not want you to see any of this.

It wants you to believe that the mind is all-powerful, that it is filled with smart connections, that it is well-organized, that it is free standing, strong, independent and autonomous. It wants you to think it is the boss.

It wants you to believe that the mind is generating its own thoughts. It wants you to believe that awareness is just some outdated artifact, that it is just a bizarre insignificant epiphenomenon of the brain. It wants you to believe in the power of the thinker, that it creates causes and produces effects. It want you to believe that it, and not awareness, is running your life.

What you are supposed to blindly believe is that the important central power is the thinker and his thoughts. Thoughts and the mind are what matters.

This mighty mind is like a mysterious super-computer. There is no point in even trying to understand it. No, don't even bother. It will be too much for you. Forget it! This is what the thinker wants you to believe.

But on a good day when you are relaxed and you can see with clarity your thoughts rising up and appearing slowly, you will see for yourself that each thought is rising up on its own from the benevolent neutral background of natural pure awareness. Each thought arises from it and then returns to it. One thought does not cause another. You see it is simple and effortless.

When you have investigated your mind thoroughly, your moment to moment experience will be that everything just happens. There is no thinker.

Then every day will be a good day because you are now the master. There will no longer be an ignorant self-centered "mind" running and ruining your life.

You will live as noble pure radiant awareness. You will enjoy expanded unbounded limitless wide open serene identity as spontaneous timeless Pure Being.

You will have thrown off the tight chafing chains of confining, defining, limiting thought. You will be as wide open, happy and free as the bright blue sky.

You will be fully and wonderfully human, yet you will be able to live in the scintillating splendor of the infinite depths of this natural pure awareness at the same time. You will be the consciousness of unity.

That ancient tyrant, the mind and its arrogant narcissistic false center, its dark heart, will die.

With this sacred crucifixion of the false thought-based self, you will find yourself reborn as the pure eternal Source. You will discover yourself to be pure Radiance.

The everyday needs that were serviced by the mind will then be handled automatically by awareness. You Are That. You are ever free Natural Pure Awareness.

How to Investigate Negative Emotions and Interpersonal Conflicts

Probably some of the most difficult times for you are when your negative emotions are strong and intense.

Then even if you have been having success gently noticing thoughts and bringing the background awareness forward, now that this emotion storm has taken over your subjective space, it seems like there is nothing that you can do. You will just have to ride it out and hope for the best.

The tendency is to focus on the content and on the story. But from the point of view of natural pure awareness, the content and the story are the least interesting and least important aspects of what is happening.

For example, we are camping for a day in the wilderness and a big storm comes out of nowhere. Rain is pouring down on us. It seems that our camping trip is ruined.

This is the story from our point of view. This is the content and the story from the point of view of the campers who are the characters in this story.

But what about the sky? What about the storm? What is their point of view in the story?

When we are camping, we hardly ever think of the point of view of the sky. We are obsessively focused on what we want and what we will or won't get.

But from the point of view of the sky, it is a natural event, a magnificent and beautiful event. From the point of view of the storm, it is doing the right thing. It is bringing water to the soil. It is making life on earth possible. It is because of rainstorms like itself that human life is able to thrive on this planet.

In times of great emotion, you have the power to step out of your story beyond the dualistic fixation of me versus you and me versus the storm. You always have the power to become the storm and look at what is happening from its point of view.

The point of view of the storm is the point of view of this natural pure awareness. It is the point of view of the sky of awareness, of this radiant pure ground of awareness. This radiant aware Presence is everything.

In practice, how this works is that first you shift your attention from the foreground to the background, to the space around your content, to the open ground around your story. Then you move your attention to the FEELINGS themselves.

Let go of the content and become the feeling, the negative emotion, the living energy itself. You want to feel its heart, its empty spacious open center. To do this, you become the emotion itself just as it is.

How to Work With Negative Emotions: a Cloud of Depression in the Sky of the Mind

Let's say it is the day after your camping trip. You had big hopes for that trip. You were hoping that you and your boyfriend or girlfriend could get closer under the stars. But now, thanks to that big rainstorm, your camping trip was a disaster. As a result, today you feel quite depressed.

You have a new option with this state of depression. Instead of being afraid of the pain of this depression, you can instead get to know it. You can gently, tenderly and respectfully approach it and make contact with it. You can actually touch it with your awareness.

When you make contact with it, you can choose to just hang out with it right next to it, just touching it, or you can actually go inside of it. Maybe the first few times you investigate your state of depression you will just hang out with it.

This way you will initiate the process of getting to know this state of depression. This way you will begin the journey of becoming good friends with your depression.

One of the things you will want to grasp right away is what is the shape of this depression state?

This depression state is hanging out in your inner sky. It is a thought-emotion object. It has a shape and a structure and a location. It is a cloud in the sky of your mind.

In the case of depression, you will probably find that it is shaped like a soft thick dark heavy dense cloud. So that is the first thing.

You want to become aware that this depression, as overwhelming as it may feel right now, is a "thing" or an object. It has unique characteristics. It has a definite location.

You will study the outer edge of this depression cloud. You will explore its texture. This texture may be rough or smooth.

It may be like silk. It may be like wool. It may be like wood. There are many possibilities. By being aware right there, you will know for yourself what the texture of its "skin" or outer shell is.

Perhaps you can detect its color. This is probably gray, brown or black or a mixture of these.

Anxiety might have similar colors but not anger. Anger typically has some red in it.

After you are done investigating the skin or outer edge of this depression state, now you go into it.

You go inside the cloud of depression. You do so in order to know it better. You do not go inside of it in order to change it. It is a perfectly good depression. There is no need to change it.

Your tendency will be to run away from it or try to change it because you are afraid of it. You are afraid of the pain it can bring. You are afraid of the power it seems to have over you. This will be true for any concentrated powerful state of emotion. It will feel like a threat to you and you will want to get rid of it.

It is time to make a new choice. This new choice is to get to know it. After you get to know it a little bit, then go inside of it and become it. You are that, too.

Experience this depression or other negative emotion from the inside out. Take its point of view about your story and your situation. Feel sympathy for it. Go into its wide open heart. Feel how it feels to be it. See, feel, think about yourself from its point of view.

You Can Reduce Your Mini-Tornado of Addiction

When you are swept away by a negative emotion and this leads to words and actions with negative results, you, what overwhelmed you was your story. You were materializing your content and acting out your script.

The emotion without the story is just energy. It is dynamic life force. Intense emotion is beautiful concentrated jazzed up aliveness. It is magnificent.

You see this with addiction. The addiction is fixation on an object. But when you focus on the addiction energy itself, you find that it is a universal pattern.

There is an inner vortex of spinning contraction. The type of addiction makes no difference in how it looks. It will look like an internal mini-tornado whether the addiction is about television or gambling or heroin.

When you are feeling strong craving or addiction, there is a little tornado of craving going on inside of you. Typically, it is located in the front of the body and involved the belly and the chest (up to the chin). You will most likely feel it in your gut as a compelling urge.

As you get to know it and make it conscious, you not loosen it up and get free from this addiction, you are loosening up and getting free from every addiction you have had and ever will have. You are seeing for yourself and positively identifying the fundamental mechanism behind it that is making it possible.

All of your negative emotions follow the same pattern. They are all like storms in the sky. They gather together, do what they do, and then disperse.

When they gather together, instead of judging them and pushing them away or trying to run from them, instead you can greet them in a friendly way in order to get to know them. In response, they open up to you. Right there something positive has happened.

Radical Addiction Mini-Tornado Busting Method

This revolutionary healing technique is taken from my self-help book "Awaken Your Inner Shamanic Healer."

Here's a special way to disperse an inner mini-tornado of craving and addiction. Using your focused mind, start at the top of where you can feel it in your body.

Chop through it side to side with your mind. Try to experience a sensation of tangible contact with the energy object (the mini-tornado in your gut).

Keep chopping and moving down through the little mini-tornado until it disperses or is greatly reduced in intensity. When you are done, smooth the area out with loving feeling. You can use a rotary motion with your mind. Go from the top down to the bottom.

This is an extremely powerful and practical technique. It is most useful when you are feeling overpowered by your craving or addiction. Be aggressive and attack it!

Paradoxically, when your mini-tornado of craving and addiction is at its maximum, that is also when it is the most vulnerable and most exposed. In order to impact you to the fullest, it must come forward and expose itself to the fullest. This works! If you "cut it down to size" while it is at its maximum display of power, it is your best chance to weaken it and even destroy it.

Another advantage of this addiction mini-tornado busting technique is that it works fast. You can use it on the spot in the situation that is stimulating your addiction. For example, if you have an addiction to gambling and find yourself in a casino, you can locate your inner mini-tornado in your gut area at the front of your body and start chopping away.

You will find that you can literally "cut it down to size." This is not just symptom relief. After working with this technique a few times and seeing results, you will be able to greatly dissipate your craving or addiction. This is one of the most powerful and fast acting ways to deal with cravings and addictions. It remains almost unknown in the West. It is fast, easy and effective.

Strong Vivid Emotions Are Easier to Awaken

Eventually, you will be able to enter into the negative emotional state and rest inside of it. You will be able to become it and understand it from within. You will be able to find, feel and enjoy its vivid inner "sweet spot." Whatever the emotion appears to be on the outside, its lively inner core, its passionate burning heart, is great holy silence exploding and celebrating.

Common sense says the more intense the emotion, the more difficult it will be. But that is not how it works. When an emotion is strong and vivid, even if it is a negative emotion, it is actually easier to deal with. Everything is exposed and out in the open.

Drop the object, usually another person, and return to yourself, the subject. Feel the intensity of the living sensation without reference to anyone or anything that is outside of you. Rest in the soft center of the cyclone. You may find this experience exhilarating!

You will find that these negative emotions need some thoughts to organize themselves around. So when you penetrate through the clouds, you will find thoughts which are acting as their hidden backbone or secret organizing skeleton. These thoughts were hiding behind the clouds. In this way the entire program gets dismantled. Often, there is one thought, the original thought from the original traumatic event, sitting at the very center of it all like a hard little rock of pain.

Then you can go inside the thought and deliberately bust the thought wide open from within. You explode it and then the basis for the negative emotion is gone and it disperses. You can also let go of the feelings. It is possible to feel the feelings and just let go of them.

If you can just let go of the feelings themselves, then the thoughts will go with them. You can let go of lots of thoughts all at once this way. The key is to feel the feelings with total honesty and without fear. When you feel them deeply behind and beyond the thoughts that are organizing them, when you let go, it all goes.

Negative Emotions Are Your Friends

What you find out by getting to know your negative emotions is that your thoughts and your feeling are not a threat to you. It is good to release them and let them go. That is what they want, too. But it is also valuable to study them in depth and in detail. These thoughts and feelings are parts of you. Love them.

They are rich like fertilizer in your soil. Your negative thoughts that are the skeleton for the emotions are likewise not a threat. They, too, are arising from you. You are natural pure awareness. Everything is you.

These negative thoughts and emotions are your own creations. They are your very own self. You welcome them and reabsorb them. They are arising from within you as an expression of you. They are your children.

Becoming the emotion means really getting to know it. Then you find that the subtle dualistic fixation between you as the thinker and the thought object gets dissolved. This frozen state melts. The water of life starts to flow abundantly again. Ultimately, the central thinker thought itself is seen to be just another thought that arises from the true you. The true you was you as the thoughts, emotions, space and ground.

When the thinker thought, like a pattern of depression or anger or anxiety or something else limiting, is seen to no longer be useful to you, then you drop it. It dissolves back into you, its benevolent open Source.

This thinker or I-thought was born and now it has died. It was your child. You were its mother.

It has lived a full rich life. You gave it life. Now you take that life back. You reabsorb it. Now it is gone.

Sitting In Your Story as Natural Pure Awareness

Let us return to the idea that you are upset right now with somebody, with another person, in your life.

There is a creative story that goes with your emotions.

There is an inciting event at the start of your story.

There is a past and a future to your story.

There is another person and there is you.

You are the subject. They are the object.

But more importantly, what is happening right now?

What is happening right now is that you are able to be AWARE of all of this content in the first place?

Ask yourself this question. "This awareness that is aware of my content... is it affected by my content?"

Go ahead. Ask the question. "Is this awareness of my content being affected by my content. Yes or no?"

Unless you are having a very confusing moment now, your answer will be "No." If it was being influenced by your content, then it would be a part of your content.

No, it is not affected. The pure pristine awareness that is aware of your content is not affected by it at all.

When you reflect on that, it is rather remarkable.

This means that no matter how tumultuous, painful or horrific your content, there is a part of you that is not affected by it at all. It is not affected by it even a little bit. No matter how terrible the thoughts, feelings, actions or events, this part of you, the awareness that is aware of this content, stays neutral and untouched.

It is pure and pristine. It is unconditioned and neutral in a positive supportive all-embracing way. Somehow it always stays true to itself. It stays free. It does this effortlessly. When you sit inside your story, you can become all of the positions of your story. If you sit on the ground or in the space of your story, you see this.

When You Sit Inside Your Story, You Discover You Are Playing All of the Roles and Positions

When you sit inside your story, you discover you are playing both ends of the polarity. You are playing all the roles. You are playing both sides. That is your true situation. It is true in your mind. It is true in your life.

You are the Universal I Consciousness. There is only one "I" and it is you. You are everything. You are everyone. Your "I" is everywhere. You Are That.

Let us say you had a fight with somebody. Now your feelings are hurt. You feel you their actions are wrong.

You are by yourself now and you are going over what happened. You are upset by these events. You can't stop thinking about them. Maybe you are mad at the other person. Maybe you blame them for something.

After the dust has settled, you reflect on your story. As you experience and relive your story within, the way you do this is that you play all of the positions and roles for both the subject (you) and the object (them). You are also the space in which they arise. You have to be able to hold both ends of your story, of your dualistic fixation, in order to tell your story.

As your story unfolds, it is obvious that it is about you and what was done to you. *How do you know this?*

What is it that is (a) able to hold this space for both ends of the dualistic fixation at the same time, (b) be aware of the egocentric holding pattern of the thinker, (c) make you the focus and center of the story, (d) recall and relive all of the details and drama, including backgrounds and (e) do all of this with no effort at all?

The answer is only this natural pure awareness. It is able to be simultaneously aware of your thinker at the center of your story and make other people the other thinkers in your story secondary to you. As you relive this experience, these other people are just thoughts.

Could it be that is all they are? Could it be that this thinker, this I-thought, which is placing itself at the center of the story, is also just a thought? Could it be that all of it is just thoughts, including the details of the story and the background to the story?

What if the only true reality in all of this is natural pure reality? What if all of the substance and authority that thoughts have, including the exalted ego pseudo-center called the thinker or I-thought, is derived solely and directly from ground of natural pure awareness?

Then all of this -- your thoughts, your actions, your life -- is just a dream, a waking state dream. After all, a dream is considered to be just thoughts, yet the experience of the dream is such that it seems totally real while you are in the dream and believing it.

Being Able to Be Both Sides and the Space for Thoughts Shows You Are Not a Thinker Thought

A story without this central thought character is just information. It is simply an impersonal record of what happened. But is the central "thinker thought" real?

When you find yourself caught up in a life story, notice that you are holding both ends of the story. You are being both the subject (the target or victim) and the object (the threat or attacker) in your personal drama.

If you were not already natural pure awareness, you could not do this. The thinker is not doing it. The thinker is caught up in the story. The thinker acting in the story. The thinker is the great star of the story.

When the thinker is swept away by the drama of his own story, then who is minding the store? Who is running the show? The answer is that natural pure awareness is minding the store and running the store.

Notice your story is happening in the FOREGROUND of your experiential space. Right now choose to become aware of the BACKGROUND of your experiential space. Just do it. Just become aware of the SPACE.

Notice that what has been going on is that YOU as the BACKGROUND have been maintaining your STORY in the FOREGROUND but you were not aware that you were doing this. In order for you to replay this story and hold both ends, both the subject and the object, the only way you can do that is to be BOTH OF THEM!

You can do that because what you really are is the unified background space or ground in which they are arising along with all the other elements of your story.

The only way for you to tell a story to yourself is to be the background space of natural pure awareness and then focus on the foreground exclusively so that you FORGET about the background which is making it all possible. You focus myopically on the thinker thought.

When you step away a little bit from this obsession with the foreground of your experience and open up the background, your relationship to the foreground instantly changes. It relaxes. It opens up. It lightens.

It becomes less obsessive. It becomes brighter and more lucid. You can see more clearly now. When you realize that you are the awareness in which your story is taking place, you have greater freedom of choice.

You Are the Holographic Inner Movie Theater

Before you saw how this works, you were stuck as the passive watcher of your inner movie. Now you are realizing that you are the movie theater. It's a great show. It's three-dimensional and holographic. It's in full color with surround sound. If you don't want to run a movie anymore, you now know you can change the movie. Or you can just not run a movie right now.

As natural pure awareness, you are the movie theater. When the movie running in your foreground is not to your liking, you can choose to become vividly aware of your background. You can choose to become aware of the living open space in which the story is unfolding.

Just by becoming more aware of the background and the wide open space that is already there magical things will begin to happen. It will be enough to loosen up your stories and relax your dualistic fixations. The frozen subject-object standoff will warm up and melt.

There is nothing that is more powerful than natural pure awareness. It is the source of the I-thought, the thinker who is the conceited star of all of your stories.

It is the space in which all of your thoughts and stories arise and disappear. It is the ground for all of this. It is both the foreground and the background. It is the totality and it is beyond any description.

The conflict and suffering in your life is a direct result of not being aware of how your thoughts appear and disappear. When you become conscious of the space, the background, you become conscious of thoughts.

When the background is brought forward into the foreground, then that automatically changes the foreground. It opens it up. It unbinds it. It loosens it up. It puts the foreground content into a balanced perspective. All of a sudden you can see into the rewarding depths beyond the shallow foreground.

The hidden and unacknowledged benevolent neutral background comes completely forward. Then what was difficult and problematic is seen instead as joyfully spontaneous and profoundly creative. Then the entire universe feels like it is your playground.

The obsession with narcissistic storytelling in the foreground gets dissolved. Thoughts come and go, even stories come and go. It is cosmic playfulness.

These elegant colorful dynamic happenings, like ephemeral yet brilliant works of art, come and go within a delightfully spacious benign environment of peace, happiness and effortless total well-being. In a way that is remarkably similar to the subtle workings of mother nature, internal and external patterns form and dissolve as needed, tireless, endless and sublime.

Thoughts and emotions appear like snowflakes, each one unique and different. Each one is a work of art as temporary as it is beautiful. These subjective states, these snowflakes, melt and dissipate. Such excess, such destruction, is possible because there is no limit to the super-creativity of the universe living inside of you, outside of you, as you. All is one awareness.

You're not in a state of happiness. You ARE happiness. You are Pure Being, the Essence of Real Happiness.

The Myth of the Mind and the Prisoner of Thought

The impressive widely worshiped concept of "mind" makes it seem like the mind is a vast great majestic impenetrable fortress, a mighty power in its own right.

This is convenient for the mind. It gives it more power to perpetuate itself, but this is not good for you.

It is normal for a person to admit that their mind is out of control and that it is causing them suffering. As a result, there is this notion of controlling the mind. It seems like the choices are to let your mind run wild and out of control or to try to control your mind.

But how do you control your mind?

If you are going to control your mind, don't you need to know what your mind is?

Don't you need to know where it is?

Don't you need to know exactly how it works?

If I want to cook with a microwave oven, I need to know what I can put in a microwave and what I should not put in a microwave. I need to know how to set the time. I need to know where the start button is. I need to know that looking in the microwave oven while it's on is not a good idea. That's just for starters

If I need to know that just to operate a microwave oven, what do I need to know in order to operate my mind? My mind does not come with instructions!

The confusion arises because people believe they know what their mind is. Thinking they know what their mind is, they believe their problem is that they have let their mind get out of control.

That is like saying "I have a dog and I have let it get off the leash. Once my dog was off its leash, it started causing trouble. So I need to get my dog back on its leash." But there is no leash for the mind. Everybody is looking for the leash. Nobody can find it.

The idea that we have a mind that is out of control that we are now going to get under control doesn't work at all. Just look around you. Nobody can control the mind. Nobody. This strategy is not working!

In reality, any strategy that seeks to manipulate the mind as it seems to be is literally playing the mind's game. Instead, the fundamental assumption that we know what the mind is needs to be investigated. When you study the mind one thought at a time, you realize that all you are experiencing on a moment to moment basis and on a daily basis are your thoughts.

You find out that there is no mind as such. There are only thoughts and these thoughts are ephemeral. They never last. Like white clouds in the blue sky, they just come and go.

The Mind Is a Liar and a Thief

Your mind is a liar and a thief. It lies to you all day long. Then it steals your happiness and laughs at you.

The mind is an endless story machine. It is only creative. It just keeps creating and creating.

It doesn't care if what it creates is positive or negative. All it cares it that it keeps creating.

Whether you are enlightened or not, the thoughts will keep coming. The difference will be that you will no longer believe your thoughts. If you examine them closely, you will see that they are not telling you the truth. Your thoughts are like dreams telling you what could be, but they act as if they are the truth.

That is why you want to question and challenge them. You cannot trust your thoughts. Not only that, you are not your thoughts. You won't be able to get rid of your thoughts. What you will be able to do is stop believing what they are telling you. Then you laugh at them.

When you wake up, that will be your freedom. You are not your mind. There is no mind. You are not your thoughts. Your thoughts are like an idiot half-brother who is always speaking nonsense. Every now and then he says something brilliant and useful. But most of the time it is garbage and you will need to discard it. The thoughts will not end, but their "stickiness' will end.

Pure Awareness and Your Prison of Thought

Your natural true self is totally free. It is free all of the time. Specifically, it is all of the time completely free of thoughts. Natural pure awareness is totally free of thoughts because it is the space in which thoughts are appearing and disappearing. It is the ocean in which the thought waves are rising and falling. Thoughts will continue, but you are this natural pure awareness!

I am telling you this now so that when you find that you are established in a thought-free state, you will understand that this state is not just a lack of thoughts. It is the fullness in which your thoughts have been coming and going. You are able to have thoughts, but you are beyond and behind thoughts.

The sky has clouds. The sea has fish. As spacious self-luminous awareness, you have thoughts.

You may not have seen it yet, but as long as you think you have a mind or that you are your mind, then your thoughts will be your prison. There is a magnetic glue that is being radiated by the central I-thought. Like a spider at the center of a web, it extends an invisible net that keeps the moving thoughts magnetic to each other. This is why they are so "sticky." If the thinker goes, if the I-thought goes, then the center of this mind web is gone. The mind dissolves, leaving just thoughts. Thoughts continue to stream, but they have no leader. There are thoughts, but there is no thinker.

The good news is that it is you that put yourself into this thought prison. It is you who are keeping yourself in this prison. So you can also set yourself free from this prison. It is your own doing and your own making.

123

That is the ultimate purpose of meditating on and realizing natural pure awareness. You will see the prison that you live in for what it is. You will see for yourself how you put yourself in this prison. You will see how you keep yourself in this prison.

You will see that it is all your own action. As a result, you will understand that since you are in charge of your own prison, you are able to set yourself free of it. Nobody else can do it for you. You can definitely do it. Sooner or later, that is what you will end up doing.

You will see with precision how you can get yourself out of this prison that you made. You will walk out of this prison a free human being and never look back.

Question your thoughts. Challenge your thoughts. Do not believe your thoughts. You do not need thinking in order to live. If you need a thought to live, it will show up. Otherwise, you do not need thinking at all. Your thoughts will continue. You cannot get rid of them entirely. But you will not believe them, you will not buy them, and that will be enough. If you do not take delivery of your thoughts, if you do not accept the package, then you do not have to pay the price.

As long as you identify with your thoughts and you think that your identity is based on and limited to your body, you will continue to live in this prison of your own making. When you get tired of all that and start to ask questions about it, then you will get interested in inquiry or natural pure awareness meditation.

Meditating on natural pure awareness is good for people who are busy in the world. It is possible to do it anywhere at any time. As long as you are awake and conscious of having thoughts, you can meditate on natural pure awareness. That's because natural pure awareness is everywhere that you are.

Natural pure awareness is always with you. If you find yourself in a moment where you are not having thoughts, then you have found natural pure awareness and you can just rest in it.

When you get to the place where you are not having thoughts, or the thoughts that you are having don't make any difference to you, then you are in the natural pure awareness state of effortless meditation.

Natural pure awareness IS the thought-free state. Natural pure awareness IS the state of meditation. There are NO thoughts in it. It is the effortless natural state of true meditation.

When you see this and realize it, then you will be in the state of effortless natural meditation all of the time. It will be impossible for you to not be in a state of meditation. Everything will be meditation. Then the thoughts may come and go. It makes no difference.

First you study the thoughts and their movement. Then you discover the background that is the mother of all of these thoughts. You rest in this source of thoughts. When you realize this source, then you will be in it all of the time. Then like the space that is the mother of thoughts, thoughts will be able to come and go in you and you won't mind. You will be unmoving yet you will allow the moving. It is paradoxical. This is how it works. You blend moving and unmoving. The part that doesn't move is the witness. Together they are the mother (space) and the child (thoughts).

Pure Awareness and the Myth of the Mind

The experience that we call the "mind" depends on the notion that there are many thoughts organized in a sophisticated way like a powerful computer.

This is interesting because the conventional way of thinking is that each of us has a "mind." This mind originates and coordinates all of our thoughts. It is like there is be supposed to be a central headquarters for your thoughts. If there is and you are not in control of your thoughts, it means this central headquarter is in control of your thoughts. This central headquarters is the thinker thought, the I-thought, the empirical self.

Some people locate the mind in the physical brain but other people are not so sure. Here is a summary of how the dictionary defines this word "mind."

"Mind is human intelligence or consciousness. It is believed to originate in the brain. It expresses itself through thoughts, perceptions, emotions, will, desire, memory, imagination, attention, reasoning, opinions and knowledge. A person who has lost their mind is in an unhealthy mental state. They will have difficulty functioning. They are no longer 'of sound mind.'"

The big deal about thinking in this way about the idea of having a mind is that it suggests that your mind is substantial. It implies that your mind is self-existing. It asserts that it is its own independent entity. If you are not its master, then this autonomous machine called the "mind" will be its own boss. If you are not careful, it will be your boss, too!

All of this is quite misleading. The reality of the mind is the exact opposite. There is no mind at all. There are only thoughts. Like raindrops, they keep coming.

When you closely examine your own experience from one moment to the next, you find thoughts, emotions, sensations and an experience or feeling or sense of existing. But you do not find a "mind." You may think that you do, but you don't.

In fact, no matter how hard or how long you look, you will NEVER find this "mind" that you are supposed to have. The reason for your failure to find your mind is that you do not have a mind!

What you have are THOUGHTS!

To recap, you don't have a mind, but you do have thoughts. When you don't pay close attention to your thoughts, you will think that they have an organizing center. There is no center. When you study your own thoughts by loving them and getting to know them, you will see this. You will see that the thoughts are just a form of creativity, like a Hollywood movie. You can enjoy them without believing that they are real.

The Mind Myth Is a Seductive Hypnotic Trap

This popular theory or concept that we have a "mind" produces serious damage. The resulting attitude is that looking closely at any one individual thought does not seem like a smart or useful thing to do. It seems like a waste of time. If you own a car, you just drive it. You don't dwell on the tires or the steering wheel.

What importance can one little thought have? Just one little thought is enough to cause a mountain of stress. Thoughts have immense power, but it is your power. When you believe your thoughts, you give them life.

Not only are we wrongly inclined to think that just one thought does not matter, these thoughts are coming and going all of the time. They are hard to catch!

We are taught it's this "mind" that matters. Thoughts are just a part of this powerhouse called the mind. Ah, but how do you catch a "mind" if it doesn't exist!

The thinker exists, though, and that is the secret. If you believe that you are the thinker, then it will rule you. You are not the thinker. You are the one that is giving the thinker his life and his power. You are the source of the thinker, the mother of the thinker, but you are not the thinker. You are beyond thoughts.

The myth of the mind is that there is this mysterious "entity" which is called my "mind." That exotic powerful self-existing independent computer-like thing is what I am dealing with. This is a big fat lie.

You get so intimidated by this myth of the mind that you may barely dare to look at your own thoughts in order to see what they actually are. How dare you presume to look at your own individual thoughts!

How dare you presume to see where they come from or where they go to! Looking at your thoughts and managing your thoughts is your mind's job. It is the thinker thought's job. But it is not your job.

This highly organized internal center of power called the "mind" is in charge of your thoughts, not you! Yet these thoughts are causing you difficulties big and small all day long. Somehow, you need to deal with the endless onslaught of thoughts all day long.

This need for secrecy should be familiar to you. Since the mind needs to operate behind closed doors, then something is going on. The "mind is up to something.

If you are honest with yourself, you will see that right now you are NOT in charge of your own thoughts. You are letting your so-called "mind" be in charge.

At one time, it was believed the earth was flat. People lived accordingly. Then it was discovered that our world is round. This resulted in some big changes.

If you wish to remain the slave of your mind, then close this book. Never look at it again. This book is for masters. It is not for slaves. Shut it this book now and go back to sleep. Or wake up. But do not get stuck in between. Be awake or asleep, but not between.

Effortless meditation on natural pure awareness will show you that you do not in fact have a mind. All you have are thoughts... and even your thoughts are not what you think they are. Although you should love your thoughts without any limits or conditions, your thoughts may not act like your friend. You simply cannot trust your thoughts. They do not know what they are doing. They keep coming and coming, but they do not know what they're doing at all.

Natural Awareness and the Crowds of Thought

The apparent continuity that you have in your experience of aliveness is due to natural pure awareness. It is not due to the mind. Natural pure awareness is always present. Like the sky, it provides continuity for clouds and birds and airplanes.

Like the ground under your feet, natural awareness is always present but you are not always conscious of it. You can walk here and walk there and never once think of or notice the ground you are walking on, yet it continues to support you all the same.

Yes, there is belief in a self-existing "mind." When the notion of "mind" is closely examined in any given moment, all that can be found are thoughts. The "mind" as such cannot be located or even described.

Thoughts can collect and gang up on you. This gives you the strong impression that they are organized and somehow being intelligently coordinated. They aren't.

You have been told that there is this thing called the mind that is behind this behavior of thoughts when they are in a group, so you go along with that idea.

When you feel the power of a gang of thoughts, your false notion gets reinforced that there is some kind of potent "mind" behind this gang running the show.

But all that is going on is that individual thoughts that have something in common were attracted to each other and became a crowd of thoughts. Magnetically they attracted each other with psychological physics.

When you are not in the habit of paying close attention to your individual thoughts as they come and go, it is typical for these undetected thoughts to gather together into crowds. When you ignore just one thought, then the thoughts can gather together like this. If you can, notice, challenge, love and know each thought as it arises. Don't believe it. Know it.

Once the thoughts have gathered together into a crowd, it does not take much for them to start behaving like an unruly or malicious gang.

When you are overcome by fear, worry, anxiety, depression, anger, jealousy or any other negative emotion, what has happened is that your thoughts have crowded together and ganged up on you.

They were sitting around in a tight crowd. They were not totally relaxed. Then there was a stimulus. There was a phone call, a critical word from your boss, an unexpected bill you must pay. Then your crowd of unsettled thoughts turned into an unruly thought mob and attacked you. They are not all that smart.

Thoughts about the same subject are magnetically attracted to each other. So they attach to each other tightly. It's like they are drinking buddies. It's not really all that mysterious. Like attracts like.

Even though each one of these little thoughts retains its own integrity and individuality, when they attach to each other and become a crowd, they act as one according to their common theme. They have energy. If you have not handled them individually, then you will have to deal with them as a cohesive group.

Natural Awareness and the Gangs of Addiction

If you are addicted to drinking alcohol (or to anything else), there was a time in your life when your interest in alcohol (or whatever it is) was being birthed into existence just one thought at a time. Your addiction developed with each unexamined arising thought.

In the beginning, a comfortable spaciousness was felt in your ability to choose and to say yes or no to these thoughts and to the effects produced by them.

Eventually, due to the repetition of the experience, these thoughts gathered together into a crowd. Once they became a crowd, your luxury of choice ended.

Now that they were massed into a coherent group, you found that they had gained enormous strength. So now instead of one thought when you think of alcohol or something else you are addicted to, you would get inundated by many thoughts all cohesively and coherently collected together. They aggressively rush in very fast and they hit you hard all at once.

They appear to be organized and to have an agenda. They are able to overwhelm you, perhaps quite easily. This is the state of addiction. You feel powerless and helpless. You feel controlled by your thoughts and the feelings that these thoughts are able to arouse in you.

Yet it is your own thoughts that are controlling you. In the beginning, you gave birth to these thoughts one at a time. They are your children. You birthed each one.

If you are struggling with serious addiction, this power of a group of thoughts may not sound like good news. If you have to deal with many thoughts at the same time, how is that different from dealing with a "mind"?

Whether or not you are convinced that you are and have a mind, one thing is certain. If you do not attend to your thoughts after you create them, they can stop being your friends. You must start being the master.

They can join a gang of like-minded negative or limiting thoughts, become your deadly enemy and make your life miserable from morning to night.

The good news is that when you study your thoughts and see for yourself how you created this addiction scenario, you will see that you really did build your addiction one thought at a time. Like any structure built one block at a time, it can be deconstructed one block at a time. The time to start and the way to start is to notice each thought, love each thought without conditions and challenge each thought without mercy.

Somewhere somehow you were introduced to the idea of this addictive experience — alcohol, smoking, drugs, gambling, sex, anger. Then this exposure got repeated over and over. Slowly a powerful inner crowd of thoughts formed. Asleep at the wheel, you paid the price. You totally bought into these thoughts. The life you gave them was your own. You believed them.

Thoughts with this addiction-substance theme were magnets for each other. They attracted each other and gathered together. Like thoughts attracted like thoughts. If you hung out with other people with a similar addiction, you got new thoughts from them.

Your thoughts became a crowd and then they became a gang. When your thought gang got big enough and strong enough, you found that you had an addiction.

Go back in time and remember how your addiction started. Notice that there was a time when you did not have this addiction yet. Notice that your addiction is the result of thinking. No thoughts, no addiction.

Notice how this addiction grew as your thoughts grew and collected. Notice how it gained power as their numbers increased. These are your thoughts. They are not some other person's thoughts. They are arising in your own neutral background awareness.

This study will be enormously helpful to you because this is how all human suffering develops. If you do not take charge of your thoughts, they will take charge.

Your study of how you cultivated your addiction can be the classroom where you get the lesson about the power of your own thoughts. You see the enormous importance of paying very close attention to them.

If you do not take charge of your thoughts, then they will become your master. Most people are pathetic slaves to their lying stealing thoughts. Even though these thoughts are lying, cheating and stealing, you still need to love them. They are your little children.

In order to wake up and become free in and as natural pure awareness, it is likely that you will first have to recognize that at this time the relentless onslaught of thoughts going on all day, and not you, is the master.

Natural pure awareness may sound blank, empty and impersonal, but it is not like that. It is more like your sense of identity is set free. You no longer feel like you have limits. Life is a celebration of wholeness.

You can now taste the rainbow and kiss the colors. You can hear the music of transcendental moments. You can feel the rapture of boundless blissful oceanity. The way is NO resistance. You become conscious of all of your thoughts. You love all of your thoughts. You get to know all of your thoughts. You stop believing all of your thoughts. You dissolve all of your thoughts as they arise. You let go of your thoughts as they arise. The way you let go of them is by knowing them inside and out. Then you do not believe them anymore. Then you just laugh at them. Really! You LAUGH at them!

Yet you still feel like you. When you study the arising and disappearing of your own thoughts to the point that you become free of them and they don't bother you anymore, you realize that now your sense of identity is relaxed and expanded like never before. Life is simple, easy and effortless. Life is just natural.

The stress and strain was from the thoughts. There are still challenges and there is still pain, but the suffering from negative thoughts and emotions that used to plague you is gone. You discover that your identity is unlimited and wonderfully unique. In the entire history of time and space, there has never been anybody quite like you. You are a transcendental individual. You are one with all, yet you are you.

Now your thoughts are just an abundant and amazing creative resource. You see that they are unlimited in their creativity. You live with a feeling of unlimited freedom. You live with the feeling you are boundless.

There is a delicious spaciousness wherever you go. Instead of living in darkness, it is like the light has been turned on and it never goes out. At long last, you know that you are yourself. You are happy. You know that this precious happiness cannot be taken from you for it is what you are.

Your heart relaxes and is at total ease. You are home.

Puffy White Clouds Play in a Beautiful Blue Sky

Like puffy white clouds floating carefree in a big beautiful blue sky, your thoughts playfully come and go in this natural pure awareness. What you have and what you are is this natural pure awareness.

You do not really have a mind. You have thoughts, and the only reason you have thoughts is that you are this natural pure awareness in the first place.

Just as there are no clouds without a sky, there are no thoughts without this natural pure awareness.

You are this natural pure awareness with or without any thoughts arising. Thoughts effortlessly appear in this wide open space of natural pure awareness.

Thoughts effortlessly disappear back into this wide open space of natural pure awareness. It is simple.

They cannot exist without it. As these thoughts come and go, this awareness stays right here. You are this natural pure awareness without limits or conditions.

You are the one source of all of your thoughts. Thoughts float through like clouds. You are free like the serene wide open sky. You are the clouds, too.

There is no mind. There are just thoughts arising in the pure wide open luminous clear space of this natural pure awareness. It is translucent. It is here and now. It is alive. It is creative. It is the reality.

Whether thoughts are arising in this moment or not, you are here now as this natural pure peaceful awareness. You will always be that. You are that now.

With or without thoughts, you are that. With or without thoughts, you are free and happy.

With or without thoughts, you purely feel "I AM."

No Mind No Problem

Investigate the Thinker and Expose the False Center

After it dawns on you that thoughts are not what you thought they were and they do not behave like you thought they did, you begin to wonder about the mind itself. What is the mind? Where is the mind?

When you start to wonder about your mind and what it is exactly, it is then natural to question the "thinker" who is supposed to be behind the mind and all of its unpleasant shenanigans. Who is this thinker?

You decide to investigate this thinker. Is there really a thinker? Is this thinker who I am? If I am this thinker, then why can't I control my own mind? If this thinker is me, how can I be aware of him and watch him?

If there is no thinker and no mind as such, does that mean that chaos will ensue? If I lose this precious pseudo-center, will I then fall into an endless void and suffer a fate worse than death? Will I go insane?

These are big questions and they are likely to come up for you in some form. The best way to deal with big questions like this is to take note of them. Write them down. Date them. Then continue your investigation.

You must do your own work. You must investigate your own mind. The prison of thought was built one thought at a time. It was built by you because you were not paying attention. One thought at a time is how you will deconstruct your prison of thought. Do not be discouraged. It will not take nearly as long or be nearly as difficult as you think.

As you make progress, there is a cascade effect. Your progress naturally accelerates. You gain momentum.

When it is dark and the sun has not yet come up, you muddle around in the darkness as best you can. But as soon as the sun comes up even a little bit and begins to shed some light on your situation, suddenly you can see clearly many things that you could not see before. This makes a huge difference in your life.

The sun of insight does not have to be at high noon to benefit you and speed up your progress. After you see the light, it will make a big difference. You will finally know light from darkness. The thoughts operated in a dimly lit environment. As you shine the bright light of awareness on them, the truth is revealed to you.

Self-Inquiry and the False Center of Attention

There is another element in your content, though, that will require your full attention. It is not going to want you to take your attention away from it and put it on this benevolent natural pure awareness.

It wishes to be the star. No matter the cost to you, it wants to be the star. It demands to be the star.

This other outstanding feature of your moment to moment content who demands to be addressed is your "I" is your apparent experience of having or being an autonomous separate self. This trickster thought form is your thinker, your I-thought. Even if you think this thinker is you, it will not be long before you see how that is impossible. This thinker is just a thought like any other thought. Its claims are false.

Sometimes it is called the "I-thought" or the "I am the body" thought. This "I" is what your story is about. "I" did this and "I" did that. This person did this to "me." That person did that to "me." This "me" is supposed to be your body, yet your body is just a physical form.

Who is this "thinker"? Who is this "I"? Where does it come from? Is it the same as the "I" in my dreams?

Let's say my wife hurt my feelings. Now I am mad at her. Who is mad? Well, "I am mad." Who are you? Well, I am "me." Who is this me? It is me, the thinker, the apparent source and owner of all your thoughts. It is this little "I" who is hurt by this other person.

Who is this "I" exactly? Where is it exactly?

If it is the thinker, then it is a thought, right?

How does a thought get "hurt" by another person?

When you have a thought and you believe it, it can cause you stress that is felt in your body. The pain and discomfort is due to you giving life to the thought by blindly believing it and not investigating it.

If it is the source and owner of all of your thoughts, then why is it being bothered by other thoughts?

If you own something, it is under your command. When you own a car, it sits somewhere until you decide it can move. You drive it or somebody else drives it. Because you own it, it does not move until you say so. If you don't say so, then it doesn't move.

If this thinker is the source and owner of all of your thoughts, then how can it be at the mercy of these other thoughts? Something is not right here.

The Thinker Is Just Another Thought

The answer to why it is at the mercy of the other thoughts may surprise you. Yet it makes perfect sense. It provides a reasonable and logical answer.

This "thinker" is just another thought! It's kind of a special thought. Just like there is a king of thieves, there is a king of thoughts. It is the thinker thought.

It is a thought that claims authority and ownership, but claiming it does not make it so. The beggar may claim to be the king. If he dresses up like the king, we may believe him. But when we find he has only the power of a beggar, and not the power of a king, we become suspicious. We realize he is just a phony.

144

The thinker, the I-thought, is a beggar dressed up like a king. He has only the power of a beggar. He is a con artist. He is a deceptive thief stealing your happiness.

Who is the true king?

The true king, the real source and ultimate authority behind the show, is natural pure awareness. Call it Pure Being. Call it Universal Consciousness. That is what you are. You are the world. You are that.

If you catch the I-thought, the thinker, when it is first rising up, you can ask it "Who are you?" and "Where did you come from?" You are challenging the thinker.

If you get the answer "From the Heart" (or "the Self" or "Awareness" or "Silence") that is the correct answer. That is where the thinker thought, aka the I-thought, arises from. The Heart corresponds to the causal body or deep sleep and its unruffled peace.

The goal of Self-inquiry is to bring you to the depths of Silence and Peace so that you can rest there.

You confront thought after thought in order to knock them down and return to the Silence. Natural pure awareness, the Heart, the Self, the Buddha Nature, the Christ Consciousness, is indeed the source of the separate self experience or I-thought or thinker. Eventually, this is what you discover for yourself.

When you discover this, you know you are free. All that ever seemed to control you and cause you all of these apparent problems was your mind... and there is no mind. There was a thinker. Now that's gone, too.

Who Is Suffering?

Why are you suffering?

You are NOT suffering because you are upset. You are NOT suffering because you got your feelings hurt. You are NOT suffering because you are mad.

The truth is that you are suffering because you are focused on yourself to the exclusion of everyone and everything else. You are obsessed with yourself as the center of existence. You are self-important.

You are narcissistic. You make yourself the (false) center of attention. You arrogantly demand that things be the way you want them to be whether or not they are going to be that way. You would be king of all.

You are the troubled arrogant irrational star of your very own reality show. It may be a crappy stupid ugly unhappy show, but you are definitely the star of it.

How can this be? You are giving the power of your attention to this feeling or sense of a separate "I." You are dwelling on yourself, on your separate self, on the thinker, as the grand false center of everything living.

This is arrogant, presumptuous and ignorant. This is the real source of your problems. Not only are you separated from the Whole, you are dwelling on your separation. You are committed to it. You are obsessed with it. For this, you will suffer.

It is not punishment. It is you who have made it personal. It is you who have made it about you.

You have made this show all about you. But it is not all about you. In fact, it is not about you at all.

You do not really exist. You only think you do. The "thinker" is just another thought. Just as there is no "mind," there is no "thinker." No mind. No thinker. No separate I. No separate me. The thinker is a thought.

Like any other thought, if you study him and challenge him and question him, if you stop believing in him, you will no longer be giving him life. He will die.

Goodbye to the Inner Drama King or Queen

The next time you are suffering, try this neutral point of view. Does it reduce your sense of suffering?

"Even though there is pain and upset, it is happening to no one. If it is happening to no one, then even though there is pain and upset, there is not really any suffering.

There is the thought of suffering, but there is not anybody to have the suffering, to maintain the suffering, to tell the story of the suffering, to be the sufferer.

If my thoughts about all of this as MY suffering were to suddenly vanish, then there would be pain and discomfort but my suffering would be less.

It might even go away or at least become quite tolerable. Sure, I would prefer to feel pleasure and comfort all of the time, but I do not have to demand that I feel pleasure and comfort right now.

It is my arrogant demanding that is the problem here in this situation today. I am going to downgrade my demand to a preference. I am going to accept and allow everything to be just as it is. I am going to accept and allow my life just as it is right now."

What is taking place when you embrace this wise and neutral perspective is that you are making a skillful distinction between pain and suffering. Yes, you are experiencing pain. There is no denying that. When you suffer, that is something different. That is not the pain itself. That is not the immediate reaction to the pain.

Your suffering is a unwise reaction to the pain. It is an unskillful interpretation of the pain mediated through judgmental thoughts, self-pity thoughts and arrogant egocentric demanding thoughts. The thinker gets to star in a new movie about "my pain." You get to be the star. It is just so unfair what happened to "you."

You can be in pain, but that does not mean you have to suffer from it. The pain is a simple fact of life.

The suffering is an interpretation of it, a point of view about it. Pain is temporary. Pain comes and goes.

If you are caught up in the story of your suffering, you may not even notice that the pain is gone! Yes, pain will go. It always goes. Whatever comes, goes.

But if you are caught up in being the star of your story, the star of your tragedy with you as the victim, you will not notice that the pain is gone. The pain acted as a trigger so that you could ride off into the sunset of your story. It was what you needed in order to make your movie. Now your movie is the thing.

The content of your story is not the truth. Your pain was real, but it lasted only a short time. Unless you are in very extreme and unusual circumstances, your pain will just come and go. In order for it to live and last and become the source of a story, you will have to dwell on it and milk it. You will need to go inward and cultivate this pain and tie it to your many other painful events. You will get to have a "pity party." When you are done milking your immediate pain, then you can launch your story and keep that going for a long time. But it is all lies and more lies. You know it is lies.

The point is that you think you are suffering. Your interpretation of events is not just that there was pain and now that pain is gone. You did not clearly see that there was no pain... and then there was some pain... and that now that pain is gone... and now there is no pain again. The clamorous clang, the narcissistic noise of your self-indulgent storymaking covered that up.

You did not see that because you are convinced that you are suffering. You think you are suffering from other people and events. What you are suffering from is your thinking. You think you are suffering because you think you exist as the all-important center of what is going on. As this all-important center, you have a story, a saga, an epic to tell yourself and others.

Narcissus May Shine, But It Is Always in Trouble

You are not the center. You do not even exist, at least not as a separate entity. Your fundamental suffering is not from the pain of your story. Your fundamental suffering is from the pain of being YOU as a separate entity, as the self-obsessed thinker, as the ignorant I-thought. You want to be in total control and it is not possible for you. Because you want this control, your frustration is bound to be endless. You cannot control the outer. What you can do is investigate the inner.

Your suffering is from your narcissistic separation. Your situation of feeling separate is your real story. In that primal separation from the Whole, there is real separation and real suffering. Your painful situation is doing you a favor by reminding you of this arrogant and unacceptable separation situation. You want to blame others for your pain and suffering. Deep in your heart you are tortured by this primordial separation.

The self-centered star of the false "I" show must die. Then the separation ends. Then the tortured heart finds peace. Until then, the search will not be over.

You can search everywhere outside of yourself but you will not find it. That's because the secret stash of true pain is inside of you. It is the separation in your heart.

Until then, the Star of Narcissus may shine, but it will always be confused, troubled and alone. A desperate dirty child living in a toxic dump of negative thoughts, it wanders aimlessly, crying in a wilderness of its own making. It is the stranger in a strange land.

It has no idea where it came from or who it is, yet it presumes to star in the show and to run everything according to its latest whims. This is arrogance, pure and simple. Like a child, it thinks that by resisting the universe, it can make it change its course. But the puny ego cannot defeat the universe. The universe ALWAYS wins. The ego will lose. The thinker will lose.

When the King of Awareness returns and the lucidity of natural pure awareness once again reigns supreme, everything will be good again. But until then, there will be trouble. It cannot be any other way. Just as two plus two equals four, negative thoughts plus more negative thoughts can only add up to more suffering.

The source of all of these negative thoughts must be identified and eliminated. Until then, you will be the slave of your own mind and suffer at its cruel indifferent bloodthirsty hand. Though the thoughts keep coming at you, the products of an endlessly fertile dream machine, understand that they are lies.

It is the mind that creates weapons of destruction in order to achieve world peace. It is the mind that says day is night and night is day. It is the mind that doubts. It is the mind that deceives. It is the mind that is afraid. It is the mind that claims to know when it does not. It lies, cheats and steals as a way of life.

The mind can see but not far enough. As a result, it keeps getting into trouble over and over again.

When you restore natural pure awareness to its rightful place in the foreground of your experience, you regain your clarity. From clarity arises charity.

You act from the vision of correct knowledge. Your life is aligned with the harmonious whole. Life is lived without effort. It is the mind that created the notion of work, the idea of having to overcome obstacles with force. There is only unity, only oneness. Love is all there is, love guided by wisdom and healed by peace.

You are already the radiant diamond in the dirt. You do not have to create the diamond. All you have to do is remove the dirt. Take off the mud and refuse that is covering the diamond. Then you are the diamond.

The nature of this flawless thought-free diamond wholeness is inherently pure, good, abundant and benevolent. You discover your existence as the cosmic Fullness of Being. This natural pure awareness is you.

When it is revealed in all of its glory, you will be amazed that such magnificence could have been so humble. Yet it was and it is, and that is part of its indescribable grandeur. It is beyond great.

No Mind No Problem

The Narcissistic Core and the Architecture of the Ego

There is a famous Bible quote about the fallen angel who said "I'd rather rule in Hell than serve in Heaven."

That is precisely your situation when you are the one who asserts his arrogant separation and commits to it. The hell you live is the one you created for yourself.

You may not be aware of it, but you are making a choice to "rule" and be the narcissistic center of your life regardless of the consequences for your life. You can continue in this way only because your life is unexamined. If you dedicate yourself to clear seeing, to knowing the truth, you will recognized that your ambitions have made you a slave of the grand illusion.

If instead you choose "heaven," then at the very least you must "serve." Then it is "Not my will but Thy will." If you would enjoy the most that heaven on earth has to offer, then you as arrogant narcissistic center of attention must die. No matter what your gains, they are ill-gotten, stolen from the Supreme. You will have to give them back. At death, everything is lost.

Only a few human beings attain the enviable status of film star or music star or famous author or famous artist or political leader or shy billionaire. Since those people have achieved a kind of greatness, a sweet superiority over other human beings, it is perhaps understandable that they would be self-centered.

155

But the ordinary person does not have a glorious life. The life of the ordinary person stinks to high heaven.

The ordinary person is a miserable voyeur who uses TV to spy on the shenanigans of the famous elite. He is not in the news. He is not special. He has not done much that matters. Few people care about him. He is not making a difference. He will not go down in history. Where does his narcissism come from?

The Hypnotic Narcissistic False Core

When you investigate deep enough, you arrive at the soft indulgent center of this narcissistic impulse. It has a sticky sweetness. There is a subtle sickness in it. It is silently repeating to itself "I Am, I Am, I Am...."

This feeling of separate existence is, at its root level, literally a blind ambition, a rogue toxic self-obsession. It is the heart of the beast, the narcissistic false core.

This is the raw barely conscious primal "taste" of ignorantly existing as a separate self notion. This is the deepest level or layer of the arrogant separate self sense. It is the raw naked primal NARCISSISM.

In deep meditation, this sticky soft sickeningly sweet self-adulating core may be perceived as an isolated living dynamic Golden Ball. It pulsates and hums with naive indulgent joy as it brashly roils about in its own self-congratulatory existential juices.

"I Am!" it cries. "I exist!" it shouts. "I adore myself," it concludes. "Is there anywhere one who is like me? I am special. I am unique. I am the one and only me like me. There is no other like me. Behold... ME!"

Yet like a baby it is blind to the road ahead. This path of self-worship is a slippery slope indeed. The price of separation will be paid many times over.

This sticky soft sweet "taste" of naked virginal separation has just emerged from the universal "I Am" consciousness. It still feels the mindless oceanic ecstasy, the ineffable cosmic lubricity of that great oneness. Now it is lost, separate, confused. It is the blind frightened essence of narcissistic self-worship.

Until it is confronted and dissolved, it secretly runs the person's life from behind the scenes. It runs the show even though it does not know what it is doing or why.

The journey of waking up makes this narcissism aware of itself. It wakes it up to a universe that is greater than itself, to a truth that is nobler than itself, to a lover that is grander than itself. It is awakened to the power and reality of humility and surrender. It finally admits that all of its power, including its separate power of will, comes solely from the Supreme.

The Inner Superstar Victim Layer

Above that unconscious sticky sweet root center of raw narcissistic self-adulation are found subconscious primal thought patterns like "I am a victim" and "Life is unfair." This is the "poor me" state of the ego.

The flip-flop alternative state is to be triumphant, to be on top. "I am the king. I am the queen. I am a billionaire. I am a famous artist. I am a famous star."

There are only two basic positions for the ego: top dog and bottom dog. Life being what it is, for the vast majority of people the only position realistically available to them is some variation of bottom dog.

Since only a few people in our society are able to attain lasting recognition as a star or person of great wealth or power, if the narcissistic separate "I Am" center for non-stop absolute self-obsession is going to make itself a star, it will have to be a bland pitiful star. They will star in some dark dismal drama, in some elaborate convoluted personal hades, in some pathetic pointless play about personal powerlessness.

Then, once again, the ego gets to be the shining star of the show. It gets to be the main attraction. It gets to be the (false) center of gravity. Only now its starring role is that of self-pitying unfairly treated victim. Oh, what a great many splendored role that is!

Yet what we see in real life is that victim and abuser can easily flip-flop in their roles. It is not about who is passive or who is aggressive. Deep down, extreme aggressors feel like extreme victims. It turns out that murders and other dangerous criminals feel that their actions are justified because THEY are the victims!

Victim or abuser or both, there is a deep feeling at the core for all who play the bottom dog in life that they are without question a terribly abused victim. They have been treated with a special unfairness. It is not fully appreciated, especially by the victims, that this is true for both the apparent victim and the apparent aggressor. Whatever the outer role they play, deep inside they feel like a helpless powerless victim.

This VICTIM layer is just above the narcissism level. In the deep NARCISSISM layer, regardless of the story of suffering and the role played in that story, this self-indulgent arrogant fixation at the center goes on. Victim or aggressor, both are acting from their toxic narcissistic core. Both are high on the drug of ego.

The Toxic Shame Layer

Further removed from the narcissistic core and just above the victim layer is the toxic SHAME layer.

There are many good books about shame and its toxic effects. The main point of shame is that you learn that there is something bad or wrong with you. Instead of you did or said something bad, you ARE bad. There is a huge difference between the two points of view.

If you have not thoroughly investigated these levels in yourself, it is a good idea to do so. The most useful study of shame in family systems may be *Healing the Shame that Binds You* by John Bradshaw. Other works by him are also recommended. Bradshaw approaches shame and related issues from a spiritual perspective.

Guilt, self-judgment, self-condemnation and other negative emotional strategies also play a role, but the architecture of the ego is that NARCISSISM is at the core. This core seeks to express itself as top dog or bottom dog. Either way, it crystallizes into VICTIM (as target or as aggressor or as both) in a starring role. Above that is the SHAME layer. It develops based on your unique personal family system dynamics.

Even when nothing can be found in the way of shame, guilt or lack of love, there is the underlying pattern of narcissistic victimhood. It cannot play anything other than victim for it truly is lost and abandoned. There is Something Else (the Other). It is God or Source or the Supreme as felt, seen and heard through the filter of the biological mother and father. The ego, the victim, the narcissistic core, is small weak puny naive child.

The core level of narcissism is not social nor is it in relationship to others. This is the primal narcissism in which the pure "I Am" of Being steps down into vast ignorance in order to enjoy naive self-adoration. This step is a precursor to a spiritual fall from Grace as the willful body-identified thinker-decider-doer-agent ego.

Polluted Confusion and Innocent Separation

You may wonder why the victim rather than shame is next in line above the self-adoring narcissistic core.

When a person has worked through most of their issues via a path of self-love and forgiveness, the layers of shame, guilt, resentment, rage, judgment and fear will dissolve. The underlying ego architecture of the narcissistic self-pitying victim is then exposed.

Until the arrogant pseudo-identity, the thinker, is dissolved, there will still be the tendency to experience the false center or separate self as a victim. To be a victim, whatever your position in society and level of success, is the fundamental ego architecture. The stories that are devised will never be sustained as tales of victory. Victory is a fantasy. Victory is for Hollywood. The Hero's Journey is ego candy. There is no hero. Confusion morphs into aversion and greed.

The beating heart of that victim structure, that which gives life to it, is the pure primal core of narcissism. It is not different from egocentric demanding. It is saying "Look at me. Behold me. I am the center of all. I worship at the altar of myself. I am all that matters."

This dimwitted narcissistic position automatically feels like the victim because it emerges in absolute isolation in a vast overwhelming field. It cannot help but feel small, insignificant, overpowered... like a victim.

If we as a drop of pure narcissism emerging from the great I AM could maintain a static state of elementary confusion, no serious problem would develop. Merely to be separate does not justify a life of suffering. The confusion leads to new developments. This is the one way ticket to the killing fields, to the blood sacrifices.

When the state of egocentric separation as the thinker or I-thought first emerges in the womb, it is not an abstract or intellectual experience. It has very distinct flavors. There is first confusion, then reaction to it.

The subjective repercussions of feeling that one is now permanently separate from one's source may include emotional tonalities of abandonment, isolation, loss, confusion, disorientation, bewilderment, condemnation and being profoundly lost in a wilderness not of your own making. The confusion is itself painful. The newly formed ego cannot stand it. It immediately panics.

In deep meditation, you may experience these original states of primal disorientation. If you do, abide there and learn all that you can from it. You will realize that they live on beneath our conscious confusion and fear.

This is the condition of the ego center just after it emerges as a separate entity but before it engages in dualistic fixation as a human child. If it is consciously accessed as a result of spiritual work, it can be a self-liberating aware state that acts as a precursor to awakening. Some people who awaken describe a state of overwhelming darkness and hopelessness that precedes the spiritual breakthrough of enlightenment.

These states of confusion after the emergence of the narcissistic seed do not remain innocent and naive. As soon as one end of the polarity is assumed by taking a strong position in separation, these states of naive ignorance transform into the blind momentum of me versus you. This "me" is at a disadvantage in the power exchange. Its victimhood begins in the womb.

Since these psychological transformations take place in the womb, at birth, during infancy and in early childhood, the nascent ego center is often subjected to convincing scenarios of powerlessness. A baby, for example, is completely dependent on its mother.

While this is the natural situation, from the point of view of the narcissistic core, the message is that you are profoundly powerless and helplessly subject to the irrational whims of vastly more powerful Others. As a result, the next layer that develops is the victim layer.

Established psychologically as a victim long before it could have chosen otherwise, the ego entity strives to negotiate its survival with these powerful other ones. Out of many possible archetypal unfoldings, personal strategic layers emerge as "my" fear, shame and guilt.

It is tempting to feel sympathy for the ego entity, for it had little chance to become other than a victim. At the narcissistic core, the person is actively engaged in arrogant egocentric demanding. They are convinced that they are superior to all persons and condition.

It is for this reason they suffer. If they did not worship themselves, it would not matter if they were victim or victor. Then all would be accepted unconditionally as God's Will, whatever happened. But they will not do that. They choose to rule in hell rather than serve in heaven. At some level very deep down, they know this is true. They know they are "sinners." Separation from God is the "original sin." In cosmic consciousness we are redeemed, for only the Light of the True Self can reach down into the depths of the narcissistic core.

Sometimes when people are drunk or in shock or afraid for their life, they will admit to this. This is not usually enough to change them. This inner knowing of the truth about one's self as separate entity is always at some level known. When it comes forward, it is realized consciously. Separation is sacrificed. Illusions of agency and free will are surrendered, dissolved by the divine power. It was all just a strange dream.

The Glorious Happy Ending of Your Suffering

Your suffering comes to an end when your arrogant egocentric demanding comes to an end. When this narcissistic arrogantly demanding self-indulgent core finally dissolves, personal suffering ends. There will still be pain, but suffering as most people know it will be gone. You can have pain without a sufferer, but you cannot have suffering without a sufferer.

This suffering entity is identical to the thinker or the thinking entity. This thinker claims the physical body as its basis. It is the I-thought, the empirical self.

Since the thinker is just another thought, it had to identify itself with something more stable and solid. Its anchor or home base became the human body. But it is all an illusion, a fantasy, a dream, a toxic trance.

Although the Victim layer is easily perceived, most people will need to work through their Shame/Guilt layers. They may also need to work through their apathy, blame, regret, rage, doubt, fear, anxiety, skepticism, cynicism and more.

Shame is a good place to start. As you keep digging the Victim/Self-Pity layers get exposed. We learned how to be unhappy. Then we used the unhappiness to try to get what we want. The answer is to be happy. Then you have what you wanted in the first place.

After you successfully expose your Shame layers, then the Victim layer gets revealed. After you work through and totally expose your Victim layer, then your primal core of self-indulgent root Narcissism will be revealed. In a way, it is like a super-massive miniature "black hole." As a black hole, it is enormously magnetic.

To arrive at this deep inner black hole of narcissistic fixation, you must penetrate the habits of negative emotions that are in the layers above it. The emotions are like a dark murky fog shielding the hidden lair of the narcissistic core. Even though it is finally seen that this narcissism is just a thought, to arrive at this clarity you will need to work through the stormy defensive layers of self-indulgent negative emotions.

In the final analysis, no matter how big your ego storm seems to be, it is still just a tiny tempest in a little teacup. It is just a smokescreen in service to its dark deluded master, the narcissistic inner core, the magnetic black hole of timeless ignorance.

The negative egocentric emotions, such as self-pity, act as a clever cloud of strategic confusion, a heavy fog. You must penetrate through them and sacrifice the dualistic fixation that supports them. This means you must own everything as yourself. You must take responsibility for everything. There are no exceptions.

You will need to give up feeling sorry for yourself. You will have to let go of your sympathy for yourself as a victim versus your abuser or attacker. All is you. All is upon you. You are responsible for your experience.

You are the ground for both subject and object. In this understanding lies your freedom. When you give in and pity yourself, you give your power to your abuser.

This is not a metaphor. Only by claiming complete and total responsibility do you get your freedom back. You will need all of your power to gain your freedom. Any power you give to another sustains the dualistic split.

To claim this freedom you will have to sacrifice the habit of favoring you as the subject over the object. You are both and neither. You are the source of both and you are beyond both. You cannot blame anyone. Your karma is your own. What you have you earned, both good and bad. Through the mind, you created it.

The instant you see this truth in any situation, you are free of that situation. You are the whole. You are all.

You are set free because it is already so. As soon as you drop your obsession with the foreground of your experience and with yourself as the exclusive center, the pattern of dualistic fixation cannot be maintained.

It depends upon the energy of you as natural pure awareness to exist. Both the subject and the object owe their existence to you, the humble pure ground. When you drop self and other to allow all to take place in yourself as the whole, as the primary all-embracing ground and sky, you melt the dualistic freeze out.

After you see the I-thought, the arrogant ignorant narcissistic contraction or distortion at the center of your suffering for what it is, all you will need to do is persist in your investigation until it is finally dissolved.

The ego or separate self sense or I-thought will wither on the vine when you no longer feed it. Now that you have seen it for what it really is with absolute x-ray clarity, you will have no desire to go on supporting it.

Since it exists only in a state of separation, if you do not keep renewing it every day and giving it life, it will die through sheer neglect. When you stop feeding it, it fades away and dies. Ironically, its brazen separation could be maintained only via a lifeline from Truth.

When you turn the full power of your spotlight of awareness upon the shadow of the I-thought, it will dissolve away. It existed because you were ignoring it.

Your awareness wakes up and becomes conscious of itself. It remembers that it is the only true basis for the feeling of being. It is the authentic identity. It recognizes itself and it feels boundless and free.

To use an analogy from pop culture, the narcissistic false core or separate ego is like a vampire. It lives in darkness and feeds on your blood (attention). Without your life force, it will fade away. Exposed to bright sunlight (truth), it burns up and dies. Though it had appeared solid, now it is gone as if it never existed.

The essential key is that you must see it for what it really is. That usually requires studying your thoughts and getting down to the source of thought which is natural pure awareness. You must know yourself.

Then you will be able to see how the narcissistic thinker thought rises up from pure awareness. Then you may see how this I-thought or thinker shoots up from the Heart up to the head and spreads its lies of illusion. When the thinker dies, you will become free.

The Mother of Everything, the Pure Ground of Awareness, Takes Care of You Now and Forever

The basic practice of meditating on natural pure awareness is very simple. You want to become consciously aware of the ground state of this natural pure awareness. You want to become consciously aware of what already is here.

As your thoughts and emotions and sensations come and go, there is something else that is always there, always here. That something is the ground or basis or foundation for all of your experiences. That something is natural pure awareness. That something is YOU.

You can challenge, confront, question or investigate your arising thoughts. Definitely do not believe them!

This benevolent neutral background never calls attention to itself. Even so, when you choose to give it your attention, it responds to you and comes forward.

Your experiences are always changing, but this natural pure awareness does not change. Thoughts change, thoughts come and go, but there are no thoughts anywhere to be found in this awareness.

This natural pure awareness is the solid unchanging foundation for everything. Most meditation techniques have you do something. That takes you away from natural pure awareness. In natural pure awareness meditation, you start right here. You stay right here.

There is nowhere to go. You are already there.

As you notice your natural ground of pure awareness more and more, you make important discoveries.

Natural pure awareness will come forward. Thoughts will get small and recede in the distance. Thoughts are reduced in their importance. It begins to dawn on you that the real power lies in the benevolent neutral background, in the natural pure awareness that in the past you had ignored as being unimportant.

As natural pure awareness comes forward, you will find peace. After you find peace, happiness, love and all of the good things in life will follow. You can and will still have your thoughts, but they will be in harmony with the rest of you. You will love your thoughts. You will laugh at your thoughts. There is no mind, but thoughts arise as if from a crazy non-stop story machine. Good or bad, it just wants to create.

Thoughts are useful and have their place, but you need to be the master. You must become the master.

As you become intimate with your thoughts and your thoughts become your friends, you will be able to see for yourself that your thoughts come from and return to this natural pure awareness. Thoughts are part of life for a human being, enlightened or not.

You will also see that the I-thought or thinker that you thought you were was just another thought. It is not a source of thoughts separate from the natural pure awareness. It, too, arises from the natural pure awareness. For a mysterious reason, it was granted a power to reign in darkness and spread confusion. Now it's reign of terror is over. Now only the sun shines.

When the I-thought or thinker finally returns to the ocean of natural pure awareness, then the impression that there is a mind dissolves along with it. The I-thought or thinker that seemed also to be a decider and a doer (agent) was the false idea that was holding the illusion of having a mind together. When it goes, the fantasy that there is a thing called a "mind" goes.

It was the string that seemed to hold the bundle of thoughts tight, giving the impression that there was one object, the mind, instead of a bunch of unique independent original thoughts. When the I-thought or central thinker string is cut, the thoughts disperse. It is seen that the bundle was just temporary. It was a collection of thoughts bound together by another thought. This temporary gathering together had no autonomy or independence. It was always only just a bundle of thoughts bound by another strong thought.

The life of this bundle of thoughts called a "mind" came from natural pure awareness, the True Self. It may not make much sense, but that is how it is.

Even though the situation is that thoughts like clouds just come and go in the wide open sky of natural pure awareness, of radiant spaciousness, the persistent illusion of a false center made it seem like something complex, difficult and confusing was going on. But it was all just smoke and mirrors. The arrogant thinker thought is a master of illusion. He is a magician.

Like the bad guy in a movie always causing trouble, this tyrannical false center seemed to always have an agenda of stirring things up and making life difficult.

When this false center goes, everything relaxes. Then you effortlessly enjoy the wide open spaciousness of the inner benevolent sky. This sky is always smiling.

Then life is simple. Life is good. Life is filled with God or, if you prefer, with Truth or Peace or Happiness. These are capitalized because they are permanent. You find that they are your very nature. They don't go away because they are what you are. You are that.

You have found your natural true peace and freedom. Your entire life blossoms to reflect your inner richness.

As the mother of everything, natural pure awareness in its great wisdom takes care of everything for you. At last, you are yourself and your life is your own. At last, you are home. You have found your true heart.

Welcome home, beloved!

Meet the Author

RAMAJI

Ramaji teaches Advaita and non-duality in the San Diego, California area. He has been a devotee of Kali Ma since She spoke to him at the Hollywood Vedanta Society Temple in 1982. He is easily reached via email or his web site Ramaji.org.

Ramaji works with students all over the world via email and Skype. He currently has students in Brazil, Australia, Thailand, United Kingdom, Japan, India, Canada and the United States.

Although there is a small fee for RASA transmission, the personal spiritual coaching and ongoing non-dual dialog he provides to his students is offered on a love donation basis.

He teaches Self-inquiry in the tradition of Ramana Maharshi with a non-dual Tantra and Kundalini twist. His work includes guiding students in the investigation of the arising I-thought, stabilization in the thought-free state and revelation of the Heart on the right.

Ramaji also provides support for people on devotional paths with Divine Mother, Kali Ma devotees especially, and for awakening Kundalini experiencers.

Via telephone, Skype or in person, he offers RASA (Ramaji Advaita Shaktipat Attunement). This spiritual attunement opens the Crown chakra to descending Grace of Divine Mother for rapid awakening of your enlightenment. Some people experience this radiant spiritual download as a white or golden light.

As the Crown chakra opens, identification with the physical body is greatly reduced. A brightly glowing wide open Crown chakra is a characteristic of the enlightened person. It is a sign that body identification is dropped and the separate will is surrendered.

Many Blessings in the One Supreme Self,
RAMAJI

Ramaji.org

Meetup.com/Ramaji-Satsang-Group/ (local San Diego meetings)

YouTube Channel: Ramaji Satsang

Email: satsangwithramaji@gmail.com

No Mind No Problem

No Mind No Problem

No Mind No Problem

No Mind No Problem

Made in the USA
Middletown, DE
06 November 2015